Making Fancy Birdhouses & Feeders

Charles R. Self

 Sterling Publishing Co., Inc.   New York

To Frances, who has had to put up with the process of getting a book ready to write, and written.

Edited by Timothy Nolan

Library of Congress Cataloging-in-Publication Data

Self, Charles R.
    Making fancy birdhouses & feeders / by Charles R. Self.
        p.   cm.
    Includes index.
    ISBN 0-8069-6691-2.   ISBN 0-8069-6690-4 (pbk.)
    1. Birdhouses—Design and construction.   2. Bird feeders—Design
and construction.   I. Title.   II. Title: Making fancy birdhouses
and feeders.
QL676.5.S38   1989   88-19215
690′.89—dc19   CIP

                              9   10   8

Copyright © 1988 by Charles R. Self
387 Park Avenue South, New York, N.Y. 10016
Distributed in Canada by Sterling Publishing
℅ Canadian Manda Group, P.O. Box 920, Station U
Toronto, Ontario, Canada M8Z 5P9
Distributed in Great Britain and Europe by Cassell PLC
Artillery House, Artillery Row, London SW1P 1RT, England
Distributed in Australia by Capricorn Ltd.
P.O. Box 665, Lane Cove, NSW 2066
Manufactured in the United States of America
All rights reserved

Sterling ISBN 0-8069-6691-2 Trade
               0-8069-6690-4 Paper

Contents

INTRODUCTION   4

1 Materials   5

2 Power Tools   13

3 Hand Tools   27

4 Jigs and Aids   35

5 Birds and Their Appetites   41

6 Birdhouse Designs   47

7 Bird-Feeder Designs   81

8 Bird Aids   99

APPENDIXES   109

A Stanley Tool and Wood Charts   110

B Wood Suitability   120

C Nails   122

D Birdhouse Size Requirements   124

E Metric Conversion Chart   126

   INDEX   127

Introduction

There are a number of reasons for having birds visit one's home, but mine is quite simple: birds liven a dead winter landscape in many ways, all of them enjoyable. Since I also enjoy woodworking—as much as I enjoy the birds themselves—making birdhouses and feeders combine two fine pastimes into solid, long-term enjoyment.

These projects show the woodworking aspects of making birdhouses and feeders that not only attract birds, but are attractive in themselves. Creating a wood project that's interesting to yourself and others, not to mention the birds, can also carry its own special pleasure.

You should also consider designing birdhouses and feeders on your own. Originality is almost more fun than slavish imitation of another's designs. Feel free to also make any changes you wish; then enjoy the results even more. Use the basic measurements and your knowledge of woodworking to make rough drawings that can be either totally new or slightly derivative.

In my first book I was limited to covering only very simple birdhouse designs in the simplest possible manner. Time, the success of *Making Birdhouses & Feeders*, and the growth of my tool collection have removed some of the constraint. I've also had time to develop a few more complex designs, even though my artistic talent—or lack of talent—has kept the plans fairly simple.

You should, I hope, find the directions easy to follow, while the chapters on tools should help you fill any gaps in your present inventory. These chapters are meant to be selection guides: actual "how-to" instructions are included with the projects, except for the very basics, for example: how to set up a table or scroll saw.

No one should take the need for me to shoot photographs without appropriate safety devices in place as an example to be followed. To get clear pictures in a number of places I had to remove blade guards and other protective devices, but you should *follow standard and common safety procedures,* as I do when I'm not shooting photos. When I am shooting, I'm even more conscious than usual of how many inches my fingers are from the blade, the chances of kickback, and so on. I never allow fingers to ride closer than six inches at such times, and always make certain that my body is well out of the way of flying wood or chips.

Get the materials and dimensions right and almost any birdhouse or feeder will attract birds. Great art isn't necessary to make useful working drawings—my drawings are certainly proof of that.

I hope you enjoy the houses and feeders as much as the birds.

1
Materials

It is possible to go into paroxysms of joy over the characteristics of wood as a material for construction, but suffice it to say that for 99 percent of humankind's needs, wood is a premier building material, whether used for shelter or a small project that gets the kitchen mugs out of the cabinet and onto the wall (Illus. 1). Wood is suitable for most uses, and the chart on page 120 covers more than you'll probably need, but may be curious about using.

Pressure-Treated Wood

Pressure-treated woods dominate the outdoor-use wood markets these days, and with good reason. The only possible hazard with them is in the cutting, during which you should make certain to cover yourself, with gloves and a face mask, to protect yourself from inhaling the sawdust.

The range of chemicals used in pressure treating is great, but for our purposes the chrome-arsenic compounds are the best. When wood is treated to a retention factor of .40 with such compounds, it is suitable for virtually any outdoor use, and treatment to a retention of .25 produces a wood suitable for all exposures except in-ground use. You will find a wood that retains its properties, yet lasts indefinitely.

One basic mistake made by many users of pressure-treated woods is that they expect it will not check, crack, warp, cup or do any of the other nasty things uncoated wood is apt to do. Well, unfortunately, that isn't the case. Water can still enter wood grain, especially at end grains (such as post tops), with all the resulting problems. (The water will freeze in winter, which will split the wood given enough dampness and time.) Pressure-treated woods are resistant to insects and rot, not to general weathering. So, if the surface is left unprotected, you can expect the wood to react by checking, cracking, and general weathering.

Illus. 1. Two useful woods: A redwood board being clamped to a piece of waferboard to serve as a guide for a circular saw.

Usually, pressure-treated woods will weather to a fine shade of grey in relatively short order if not coated with stain or a protective water-repellent substance. Many water-repellents used today also allow the wood to weather grey, which, in light of the rather mean-looking green of most pressure-treated woods, is a good thing.

One of the great problems with pressure-treated woods is the chemicals used in assuring preservation of the wood over a long time, and their effect on the birds. Considering the compounds used, the concerns are legitimate, and I've checked with several companies in an effort to determine what precautions need to be taken.

The precautions we would take with human use seem reasonable when preparing homes and feeding stations for our feathered friends. Thus, no unfinished pressure-treated wood should be used where a bird's feathers or skin would rest against it. Such uses may not cause a reaction, but it seems reasonable to take precautions just in case the various available studies missed a point or two.

For feeders, the instructions are strict. While the chemicals are specifically designed not to leach out of the wood, pressure-treated wood is not intended for such things as kitchen cutting boards. So, the feeders must have their actual feeding area, (including hoppers), made of material other than pressure-treated wood. No type of finish will last as the birds peck away to pick up, crack and ingest their food. Eventually, small bits of wood will be ingested, and no one knows what sort of poisoning might result during the digestive process.

Pressure-treated wood may be used for birdhouses, if those interior portions where the birds will nest are covered with a varnish, paint or other material (Zar exterior polyurethane is also good if varnishes seem too difficult or not apt to last. It makes a near ideal finish coat for items to be seen as clear wood that must remain outdoors, such as birdhouses and feeders.)

The best uses for pressure-treated wood

are feeder posts and birdhouse supports. This will prevent any need of replacement for about three of four decades, assuming the material is treated for ground contact and in-ground use (a .40 retention rate).

Natural Woods

Natural woods vary widely in working qualities, such as how easy it is to drive a nail, machine the wood and apply the finish. Other qualities are also important, but if you can't accomplish these three, you're better off saving your money.

Hickory is a good example. It has an open grain, does not like most finishes (lacking, that is, some extensive preparation), is very hard, and thus is hard to machine in any way, not to mention rough on tools and expensive.

Woods like white pine, cedar and redwood are better buys. While none have the strength of hickory, all are easily shaped, take finishes well (redwood and cedar do better when undercoated), and are easily screwed or nailed, with or without pilot holes (a good idea to keep the wood from splitting). They are also relatively inexpensive—at least in comparison to hickory and white oak (Illus. 2).

In addition, redwood and cedar offer natural resistance to decay and insect damage, while white pine—and most of the other pines—can easily be treated to prevent such damage, or painted. Any of these three will suffice for basic construction. In fact, you can simply change any plan specification to read "white pine" if I specify another wood, and forget any complexities at all. Use pressure-treated white pine where resistance to decay and insects is needed, and plain white pine where it is not.

Southern pines are different animals, falling somewhere between pressure-treated and white pine. Its natural rot resistance is a bit higher than white pine's, but it's also a harder wood, a real nail bender in some species and grades, and less attractive

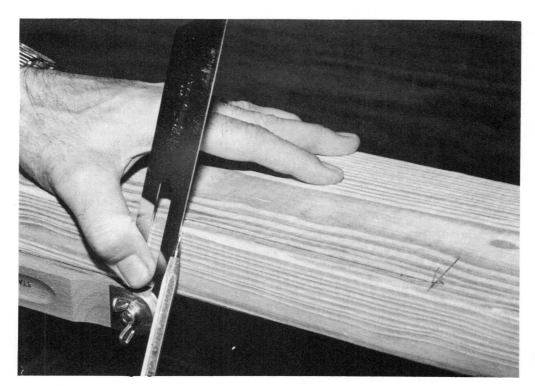

Illus. 2. White pine being dadoed.

Illus. 3. Yellow, or Southern, pine showing its characteristic strong grain pattern.

to most people. Still, for birdhouse and feeder use, it's nearly ideal, because it remains reasonably easy to work, is cheap (within its cutting areas), takes many finishes well, and is pretty durable even without coatings and treatments. Its also rugged and durable when treated (Illus. 3).

Manufactured Woods

Manufactured woods are those that have man-made help beyond simple drying, sawing, and planing—in other words, plywoods, Waferboards and oriented-strand boards.

For birdhouse and feeder construction,

only the exterior grades are suitable for use. Exterior plywood grades use waterproof glues, and for designs that specify constant water contact, such as birdbaths, marine plywood grades are preferable.

To eliminate the expense of marine plywood, you can seal all the seams with a top-grade exterior caulk, either marine or construction, and give the entire unit three coats of a good, polyurethane exterior coating, such as Zar exterior polyurethane. Thin the first coat lightly; then lightly sand the first two coats after no less than six hours' drying time. Such a treatment will provide as close to a true waterproofing as one is likely to find for constant water immersion, but even then, expect only about five years out of your birdbaths.

When selecting any manufactured wood product, choose a product graded by the American Plywood Association. For most all birdhouse and feeder uses, a B-B or B-C grade will be sufficient. Grade A faces are meant for natural finishes, and are not really necessary, as most of the plywood will be painted or coated with opaque exterior stains (Illus. 4).

Waferboard, or Waferwood™, from Louisiana-Pacific is another good wood. The glues are highly water-resistant, allowing you to use one of the sheathing grades of the board with little worry about material separation. (However, if the material is unfinished it will separate, but that's due more to the weathering of individual wood chips than a loss of glue strength.)

Illus. 4. A high-grade plywood being routed.   (Courtesy of Porter-Cable Corp.)

Adhesives

Most birdhouse joints are going to need something to hold them together. Glue is an option. Unfortunately, not one of the lower cost ones work outdoors: yellow woodworking glue is water-*resistant,* not waterproof, and is susceptible to quick failure in extreme humidity and long-term dampness. White resin glues are even more failure-prone under damp conditions, and hide glues are worthless outdoors.

When all else fails, many of us turn to epoxy glues. These are superb for most small projects, but are too expensive when used in any quantity. Their fast setting time is also a problem with the more complex projects that rely on adhesive strength for assembly and durable bonding, since slow epoxies set in ten or fifteen minutes. Keep epoxy glues on hand for quick, solid, and secure attachments in any weather, but remember its working life is short and cost high.

Unfortunately there are no waterproof adhesives that are really low cost, including resorcinols. Resorcinol adhesive does go farther than epoxy and has a much longer working life, but it also requires clamping and some special care.

Mix the resorcinol by adding the liquid resin to the powdered catalyst, and mix it for five or ten minutes. This will make it a dark tan. Apply the glue and let it air-dry for ten minutes or so; then clamp. Once the parts are bonded, you have about forty-five minutes to do any rearranging. Wipe off any squeeze-out with a damp cloth, and leave the clamps on for twelve hours (ten is recommended, but more won't hurt).

A pint of resorcinol will bond about twenty to twenty-two square feet of surface, and the relatively long pot life and long adjustment times make it far preferable to epoxy for most woodworking purposes. The glued joint will be stronger than the wood, and will resist water, insects, bacteria, fungi, and most chemicals. The joint line will be dark tan to reddish brown.

Nails

Nails used to construct birdhouses and feeders will almost always be six-penny or smaller, often as short as one inch (a brad, really), and should always be either coated to resist rust or made of stainless steel or aluminum. Finishing nails do a good job, but box nails are also useful. Box nails look the same as common nails, but have a thinner shank, so they are less likely to split small pieces of wood (Illus. 5).

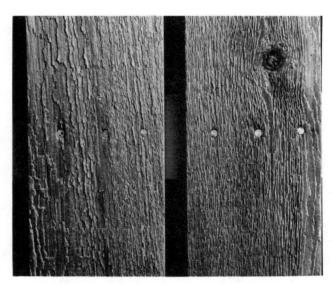

Illus. 5. Aluminum versus steel nails under weathering conditions shows that steel loses.

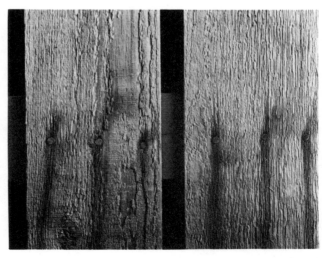

Screws

Most woodworking screws are either brass, stainless steel, or any number of platings. Most are also coated with a matt black material that is fairly rustproof, but will wear down over time. Stick with the more costly types, and you'll be fine, since you won't need that many.

Screwheads cause more confusion than any other feature on screws, so keep these things in mind. First, for most uses, either a Phillips or Robertson (square-depression) head is best, especially for power-driven screws. The reason is simple: the screwdriver's increased grip helps prevent skidding and tearing up of the screwhead. Some new screwheads have a square depression with tips that run out from the corners to allow the screw to be withdrawn with a Phillips screwdriver, although they won't *drive* with the Phillips.

Brass screws look best in whatever head style you prefer—flat, oval, or round. For general use, zinc-coated screws are sufficient. Stainless steel is the stronger and most weather-resistant, but isn't necessary that often.

Self-tapping screws are meant for power drivers, so they don't need pilot holes, which saves time. In most applications, they're excellent, but in close-to-the-edge work, you may want to drill pilot holes anyway, because a fraction of an inch of drift may send the screw where it isn't wanted.

Plastic

You'll need a sheet of Plexiglas acrylic plastic for some of the feeders. It's easy to work with, comes in a wide variety of thicknesses, shapes and colors, and requires no special setup before use. It's a good idea to keep the thin paper film on both faces when you're marking and cutting so that you won't mar this very soft material. When cutting, use the finest-toothed blades possible and keep tool speeds fairly low—the stuff melts very easily. If you can't adjust the speed, make the cuts as short and quick as possible, without sacrificing safety.

Plastic pipe serves all post types well if you prefer not to use wood posts. Generally, a DWV (drain-waste-vent) schedule 40 polyvinyl chloride pipe, two inches in diameter, will be perfectly suitable for all uses (why it's called schedule 40 isn't important besides knowing what to ask for). You may, though, find yourself dancing around a bit to find a pipe flange to fit. If it becomes a major problem, go to a 3-inch closet flange; then either use a reducer or change to 3-inch-outside-diameter pipe.

Dowels and Hinges

You'll need dowels for perches and porch railings and, in the case of the log cabin, as actual building materials. These, and the wooden dollhouse shingles used on a couple of projects should all receive a minimum overnight soaking in a preservative. Two or three nights would be even better, followed by a few days of air drying. Plain surface-mount hinges with fixed pins will suffice for any work required.

Finishes

The range of good and sensible finishes increased over my first book on birdhouses for several reasons. For one, some of the projects in this book use colorful patterns or designs on the birdhouses, while others are made of wood not naturally weather-resistant, so it needs some protection. Still others would simply look better with a coat of paint or clear finish (Illus. 6).

Proper preparation determines, in large part, how good the finish looks and lasts. Not using primer is one example of a poor solution to covering a board.

For a smooth finish, the wood should be smooth and clean. Sand carefully with 100- and then 220-grit sandpapers; then clean with a tack cloth or lint-free rag soaked and wrung out in paint thinner (Illus. 7).

Illus. 6. Zar Rain Stain opaque stain was used to finish this large birdhouse.

Illus. 8. Rain Stain being applied.

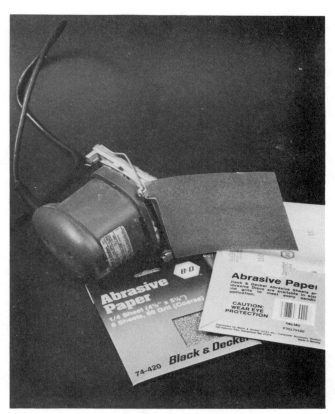

Illus. 7. Black & Decker's palm sander is fine for almost all light work, uses a quarter sheet of sandpaper that is easily attached with built-in clamps, and works well for long periods.

If you want a finish that'll last outdoors, you must use an exterior finish (Illus. 8). Using a top-quality finish will give you a longer-lasting job, and a gallon of good exterior stain, clear finish, or paint will coat as many birdhouses as you're likely to build for a while.

I've only found two clear finishes that I would consider suitable for these projects. One is water-repellent, intended for pressure-treated and other woods. Either put it on with a brush or roller, or soak the wood for as long as possible. The more repellent the wood absorbs, the better it will work, and lets the wood age naturally. Water-repellent finishes help prevent checking and cracking of woods, thus prolonging their life and attractiveness.

The second clear finish I've used is Zar exterior polyurethane finish. It comes in gloss, semigloss, and antique-flat finishes,

which will cover most needs. Thus if you design and build a log-cabin-style birdhouse, you won't have the completed project looking like a highly polished piano (Illus. 9).

Illus. 9. Leave plenty of time for the rain stain to dry.

2
Power Tools

As I said in the Introduction, this is intended as a recommendation chapter; these tools are not all required to build the projects. Remember, though, the more expert the reader, the more loose the recommendation. If you want to rip stock or do crosscuts on a table saw, band saw, or radial arm saw, do what you like best (Illus. 10).

Routers are not stationary power tools, but are very handy and can be made at least temporarily stationary for edge trimming, shaping and similar work. Once you get your router stationary you can use it as a stationary shaper-type tool, with the router bits. This is what I'm doing now, and it saves a lot of money in bits, but I'd buy a shaper if I had the space, because it is a time-saver.

Keep in mind though, that there is virtually no job a power tool can do that a hand tool can't. Routed designs can be carved, and all saw cuts possible with a table saw, band saw, or scroll saw (among others) can be duplicated with a panel saw, or coping saw. But for saving time and for reproducibility, power tools are the choice.

Stationary Power Tools

Table Saws. The basic features of any table saw are quite similar: there is, of course, the table, through which there is a slot for the circular saw blade, which is attached to a

Illus 10. Table-sawing a rip cut.

motor in any of a number of ways (Illus. 11). Straight drive saws take power directly from the motor. Heavier-duty saws take power through a series of belts that are driven off the motor pulley so that you can use a number of different motors, with different power characteristics.

You'll find a wide variety of table types, sizes and materials available. I love open-work cast-iron tables of reasonable weight,

Illus. 11. A dado being made on my Craftsman Flex Drive table saw.

Illus. 12. Wide crosscuts are simpler and safer with plenty of room in front of the blade.

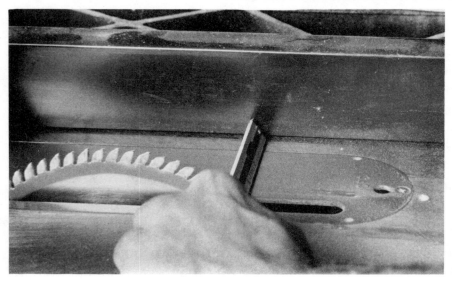

Illus. 13. Table insert. Note the screw adjuster.

because these have little or no flex under normal to moderately heavy use. A sheet-metal table, however, should be avoided or replaced as soon as possible, no matter how many ways it's braced or how good the saw it came with. A small sawing table should also be avoided.

Quite possibly the most important single table saw measurement is the distance from the front (working) table edge to the fully raised saw blade. A full foot is close to ideal. A distance of less than 7 inches limits safe crosscutting of wider boards, and safe mitring of almost any board over 4 inches wide (Illus. 12).

Stability is all-important to both accuracy and safety. A table saw that dances and wobbles on its stand is dangerous, because it's too easy to get your hand in the blade. For any stationary power tool, in fact, stay well away from a wobbly stand, and if you order any by mail, make sure you've got at least a thirty-day free-return privilege so that an unstable table saw can be shipped back. Naturally, stands can be braced, or even built, but make sure that's something you wish to do before getting involved.

As for table inserts; each and every one is a pain to adjust. The better ones are heavy enough to hold their adjustments and do not flex excessively in use. Many require a screwdriver or hex key to adjust for dado or moulding inserts, while others, most often on production style saws, can be lifted out without any detaching operation (Illus. 13). Look for good thickness and moulded-in bracing on the back of the lighter inserts. Slots, whether for dadoing or straight sawing, should be as small as possible without interfering with blade action. Small slots allow accurate cuts on thin stock with fewer worries about the stock dropping down into the slot, causing cut-deflection errors.

You can often make a temporary insert for dado blades as long as your saw doesn't have drop-in inserts. Simply cut tempered hardboard of the correct thickness to size, attach it properly using the screws from

Illus. 14. Adjusting the table insert requires care, and is essential to clean, safe cutting.

Illus. 15. Note the blade pocket width on this dado insert. (Courtesy of Delta Industrial Machinery.)

your stock insert; then raise the dado head slowly to get the proper size cutout in the insert. Even if your saw has dado inserts, insert slots are generally limited to about an inch or so across. In such circumstances, a homemade dado insert could prove of at least occasional use for many people (Illus. 14–16).

Saw power should never be less than a full horsepower (rated for the bottom figure); 1½ horsepower would be even better. If you can afford it, heavier is probably better for most full-size (10-inch diameter and up) table saws, but an awfully large chunk of the cost of a table saw is in those copper windings and steel and iron cases. Remember that stalling power, which is much higher than running horsepower, is often given as a suitable figure for motors. Believe the lower number.

Most table saw motors (even 110-volt models) will require a separate circuit. Either a small appliance circuit using #12 cable or a time-delay circuit breaker or fuse

should do the job. Heavier motors (220 volts) should have branch circuits, fused for at least 20 amps, with single outlet receptacles. If you are running two or more pieces of heavy equipment in your shop you may wish to use a single branch circuit, fused for 30 amperes, with individual switching to each tool, but check local codes carefully to see if this is legal. Since it is cheaper than running in three or more separate 220 volt lines, and you'll seldom run more than one heavy tool at a time, it could be useful, if allowed. For practical and financial reasons, no home shop should get involved with three-phase electrical power.

Table saw accuracy depends on the massiveness of the saw, the accuracy of the machining, and the technique of the operator. Almost any of us can eventually get an accurate single cut by making enough sample cuts; then repeatability and quickness of set-up becomes important as we gain practice. Adjustments are almost always neces-

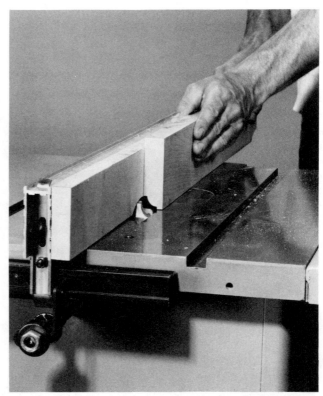

Illus. 16. Note the width of the pocket, and the special attachment to the rip fence, used on the insert with this moulding head and cutters. (Courtesy of Delta Industrial Machinery.)

sary, and fences and mitre gauges will rarely be right on the mark, so the best start is a saw that comes as close to dead-on accuracy as possible all by itself.

Although top design and production costs money, generally, when you reach a certain price range for table saws suitable for home shop use, the primary difference will be the color. Most of us are working down from these models, so we need to consider overall construction. Look for basic solidity of construction and clean castings, as well as consistent machining marks. No cable under #14 should be used, so check the cables. Make certain all switches and controls are easy to reach and operate smoothly. If at all possible, make some check cuts with the saw you buy. Check the blade, the mitre gauge, and the fences to see how smoothly they work. Keep in mind your need when testing the saw. If all you cut is 1-inch pine, there's no point in checking a saw to see if it will groan to a stop in 2-inch green oak (or paying for it). Remember that fences and blade guards can be purchased separately. You're also going to

have to get a good set of saw blades, preferably carbide-tipped (Illus. 17).

Table saws range in price from about $125.00 for lightweight models on up past $2000, by the time you add fence, stands, fence bars, etc. Make your decision based on your needs. If all you ever expect to build are birdhouses, lightweight models such as the 8-inch saws from Skil, Black & Decker, and Sears are more than sufficient, and with careful use can produce some pretty fine projects in other sizes as well. Remember, though, that it is always possible to move up in tool quality and capability if things interest you a great deal, but the market for used, expensive power tools is limited.

Band Saws. Band saws are simple tools that perform a variety of jobs well, although most will require some tuning up after you buy them. Competition is so intense that prices have come down, quality control routines have suffered, and more and more band saws have out-of-round, out-of-balance wheels, and sub-par blade guides. After about a dozen hours work and an-

Illus. 17. The Piranha blade line is shown here. Note the different shapes of the blade tips. (Courtesy of Black & Decker.)

other two dozen hours testing you will be able to do what you should have been able to do with a showroom stock band saw.

Now for the good news. Band saws will cut curves, even compound curves, in very heavy stock (impossible with a table saw). The lightest band saws will work with stock up to about 4 inches thick, and most will work with material to 6 inches thick. Some brands use a lift kit that, with the appropriate blade can cut materials up to 14 inches thick (Illus. 18). With wider blades the band saw can rip quite thick stock.

Pad cutting (holding pieces together while cutting an outline) can be done on any band saw without the limits given on other kinds of power saws. The slow cutting speed of band saws makes control simple (assuming wheels are balanced, and the blade is aligned and properly tensioned). The result is a real time savings over cutting the pieces individually, as well as the certainty they'll be close to identical, making fits with other pad-cut pieces easier.

Band saws differ markedly from other power saws, using two or three wheels to

Illus. 18. Delta's 14-inch throat depth band saw model is probably one of the best buys in band saws around. (Courtesy Delta International Machinery.)

guide the saw blade. There are a number of three-wheel models (Illus. 19), but I am leery of any band saw using such an extended neck design, because it simply *cannot* be as stable as a solid shaft of iron or steel. As with most tools, stability is very important, and once basic stand stability is taken care of, the remainder must come from within the design of the tool. A solidly built neck is important on a band saw, as is a heavy table of cast iron or aluminum (preferably cast iron). Still, there are certain trade-offs that may be worthwhile. Some

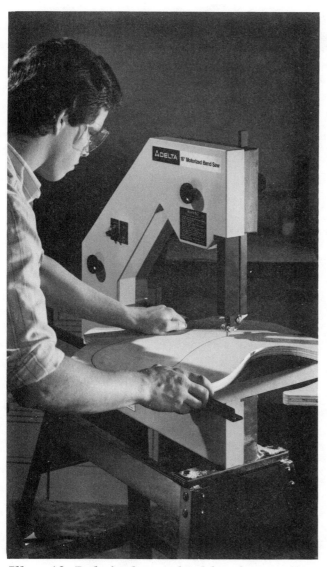

Illus. 19. Delta's three-wheel band saw offers greater throat depth, at lower cost, than any but the most expensive commercial band saws. (Courtesy Delta International Machinery.)

ease in lowering blade speed will allow metal cutting, as well as great throat depth at modest cost, and make up for a possible (and, honestly, conjectured) slight lack of stability, and shorter blade life (the blades have to turn sharper corners in three-wheel band saws, so they break more often).

A band saw table is quite small compared to a table saw's: about 13 to 15 inches square. This is sufficient for most work, and extensions are available (at extra cost) for more specialized cuts (long cuts, rips, etc.).

The pivots that support a tilting table need to be massive, but easily adjustable. The table should move easily in its tilt guides and tighten solidly without your having to exert enough force to move a wrestler across the room.

Cast wheels of iron or aluminum are probably best for all band saw uses, and some makers balance and true the wheels at the factory. A band saw's power is not as great as a table saw's. There is less blade to drive through the wood (few band saw blades are over ½ inch, though they do run up to three inches, which needs a more powerful motor). Most band saw motors are ½ to ¾ horsepower, sufficient power for most uses (except ripping). You'll get into power trouble if you do extended heavy ripping jobs, which most band saws aren't suitable for anyway.

Band saws start at $100, and rise to about $1,300, but you should forget the $100 band saws totally. Plastic wheels, poor guides, lightweight tables that warp and wobble and won't hold adjustment make them good only for being able to say your shop has a band saw and little else. Sensible light-duty-use band saws start at about $300 and go upwards. They're not as expensive as table saws, but then, they don't have the power. They do a number of jobs reasonably well, and cut curves in heavy, or padded, stock exceptionally well. In a pinch they can serve as a basic shop saw, though it'll never keep up with a table saw in accuracy, speed, and versatility.

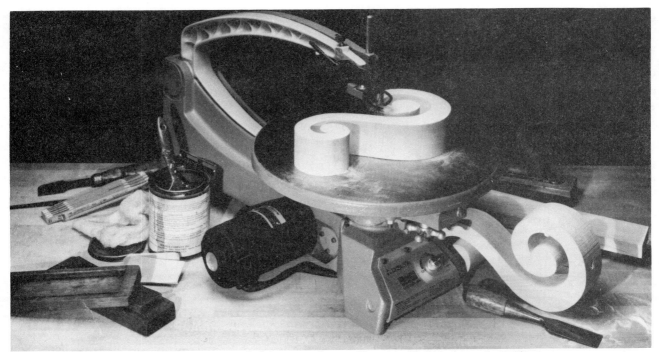

Illus. 20. Delta's electronically variable speed scroll saw. (Courtesy of Delta)

Scroll Saws. Scroll saws are woodworker's Cabbage Patch dolls. Everybody wants one and every manufacturer makes at least one. What everyone forgets is that under no circumstances is a scroll saw suitable for total shop emphasis. However, as a tool for cutting complex shapes, the scroll saw is extremely handy, while also being one of the safest stationary power tools for a beginner to use, because of its slow blade speeds, low power and small, well protected blades (Illus. 20).

Beyond these uses (and very light pad cutting) scroll saws are generally luxury items (with some costing luxury prices). That said, the scroll saw is superb for doing internal cuts on light stock (it is the only such wood saw, in fact, that works with power), and is tops for cutting letters for signs, internal designs of any kind, and, of course, fancy scrollwork (Illus. 21).

If you wish to build a Victorian birdhouse, feeder, or dollhouse, there is little other choice, except the coping saw (page 28), which suffers its own limitations (including a lack of a motor that can make for an awfully tired arm).

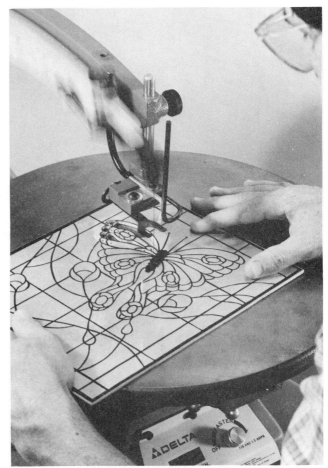

Illus. 21. Delta's electronically controlled scroll saw is one of the smoothest cutting available, and offers an exceptionally large table. (Courtesy Delta International Machinery.)

Drill Press. One of the least-noted useful tools for the home shop is the drill press. The reason it is left out is that small electric hand drills are a great deal cheaper (most of the time), and easier to use in many ways. Still, a good bench or floor drill press is not extremely expensive, and can provide drilling capacity and accuracy that may only be dreamed of with portable power tools (Illus. 22). Many companies make small bench-top models that provide ½-inch chucks, at a dozen speeds, either electronically controlled or belt driven. This is not a high-tech tool, and doesn't need to be, since high tech is extra cost to meet no real need. Aside from precision drilling, table-height adjustments to any point on the shank (or a rotation of the table out of the way), rack-and-pinion gearing, and ball bearings (for an exceptionally smooth feed), nothing much is really needed. Use this type of tool in conjunction with brad points or Forstner bits and you will be amazed at the quality of your hole-making (Illus. 23).

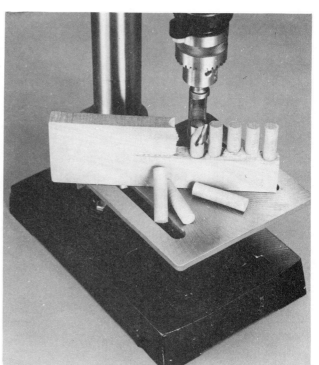

Illus. 22. (left) Black & Decker's floor drill press.

Illus. 23. (above) Plug cutters are handy accessories, and are shown here on a smaller drill press from Delta.

Jointers. The jointer is a simple tool that falls in the middle price range for power tools, and is more essential than most of us realize, especially for edge-jointing boards, (rabbeting is often easier with a router and a table saw). The jointer is the most accurate method of edge-jointing boards when a good, clean joint is needed for strength and appearance.

As with any other stationary power tool, examine the castings to make sure they're cleanly done, and check the tables for flatness, fit, and ease of adjustment. Different jointers use different table adjusters, and these require a bit of time to adapt to. The fences and guards should be easily moved, and blades should change easily so that you're not tempted to leave a dull blade in place.

For lightweight shop work, a 4-inch jointer is sufficient. For middleweight work, a 6-inch model will do, and if the table is at least 5 feet long, will do larger work. Beyond this, you're working with industrial models and prices.

When looking for size, check the width and the depth of cut. While several light passes give a smoother finish, there are times when a heavy pass or two will reduce a board's edge at the necessary speed to be followed up by light passes to finish-joint the work. Depth of cut will rarely be over ½ inch, often as little as ⅛ inch. Depth of cut is a function of power, primarily, and is not extremely useful for light jointing.

Portable Power Tools

Portable power tools encompass a much wider area of jobs than do stationary tools, and a number are quite handy for producing birdhouses and feeders. I haven't attempted to make this listing complete in tools covered, or exhaustive in the possible uses of those tools, because to do so would require another book that would be outdated before I could finish writing it. Generally, portable power tools are used for jobs that require somewhat less accuracy than is needed when stationary tools are

brought into play, and the general method of power is electricity.

Routers. Choosing a router is probably the toughest job in woodworking. There are simply too many brands, and too many styles and sizes within those brands, to make a simple selection (Illus. 24).

It is easy enough to define your needs and opt for the router closest to fulfilling them, if you know your needs and have some experience with router selection. But if you don't, it is possible to leave a very expensive tool sitting on a shelf.

My first recommendation is that you find some way to get at least a little hands-on experience with a router, almost any kind of router. A couple of hours working with different bits, cutting grooves and freehand designs, should do it. Use piloted edge bits and nonpiloted bits, and make cuts on edges and starting in center stock where the router must be plunged or tilted in. Make through cuts and partial cuts; then check the characteristics of the router (horsepower, chucks, handles, worklight, etc.) and, above all, see how it *feels* to you. Examine these features carefully, with particular attention paid to the feel, the cut and the bit. If the cut was clean and easily made in stock you commonly use, and the router felt right to you, the rest will just about certainly come in time.

Certain basic router features do make a difference. First, ½-inch collets use ½-inch shank bits, which cost more but provide greater bit-head stability and much more accurate (and usually cleaner) cutting. Second, low horsepower routers aren't good for much other than the softest of softwoods, so if that's all you use and plan to use, a low-powered router will be sufficient. Third, a router that has two horses or more isn't much better than a pro model 1½ horsepower router for mat cuts. These heavy-duty routers are really for production cutting, which you and I will probably never do.

Router handle choice is a personal mat-

Illus. 24. Router. (Courtesy of Porter-Cable Corp.)

ter, as is plunge or tilt-in cut starts on interior board surfaces. Plunge-cut routers tend to hold depths less accurately than do tilt-in routers (also known as micrometer adjustment routers). The plunge mechanisms will wear out before anything else on the machine, though some are fairly simple to replace. Plunge-cut routers do provide more accurate starts in fancier routing patterns, and are especially handy in cutting signs and specific designs. Tilt-in routers have an advantage in edge cutting, especially with repetitive dadoes, since they maintain depth better.

If I were selecting my first router, I'd aim for a decent 1 to 1½ horsepower model, preferably with a changeable set of collets so that you could use both ¼- and ½-inch bits. A work surface light would be a nice option, as would an electronically speed-controlled model to reduce stock burning. It should also have a lock for the collet.

Bayonet Saws. Over the years, I've had quite a number of these saws, and currently have two professional models that I feel are the best I've ever found. They're heavier and more stable than the "consumer edi-

Illus. 25. Porter-Cable's variable speed, barrel handle bayonet saw.

tions" that so many people buy, and which I will not have again. Consumer models vibrate too much for any form of control and are much more difficult to control (although a professional saw will still vibrate too much for really precise work or work with soft grains). If the baseplate is held firmly against the work, and the work is well supported, you'll get a good amount of control with little damage (Illus. 25).

Neither of my saws has an adjustable baseplate; so essentially, they're limited to 90° cuts (Illus. 26). Thus, for compound cuts, you'd best check elsewhere. As you may guess, I like these saws.

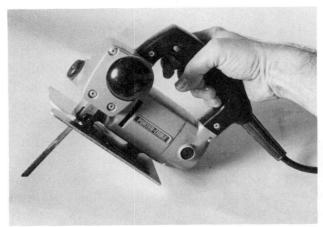

Illus. 26. Porter-Cable's top handle standard bayonet saw.

Circular Saws. A circular saw sees so much use around the average shop I cannot understand why anyone would bother with a consumer model. The difference in cost between one of the middle commercial grades and a decent consumer-model saw is tiny, but the durability and accuracy to be found in the heavy-duty model is something like ten times that in the consumer model. I can, and have, burned up top-of-the-line consumer-model circular saws of several good brands in a single day's use (Illus. 27).

In most cases, the standard 7¼ inch is sufficient for all work at hand. I have smaller and larger types, but they get little use. Always try to use the greatest number of teeth possible to provide the smoothest

possible cut, and carbide-tipped blades are preferable. They cost more to buy and get sharpened, but they last a lot longer, thus reducing wear and tear on the saw arbor, bearings, arbor nut, and your nerves.

Professional model saws have thick baseplates that give the saw more stability. I also like drop-foot baseplates, those that simply slip straight down for depth adjustment. Large handles and knobs will also make control easier. Most pro style saws have a very heavy power cord that is usually 10 feet long, so that the plug won't get hung up when you make long cuts.

In most cases, you are not getting enough saw for your money if the saw draws under 12 amperes. Some draw a full fifteen, and this will require a separate circuit.

Drills. For most work a drill with a ⅜-inch chuck is more than sufficient, and for really fine work either a drill press or a ¼-inch

Illus. 27. Porter-Cable's Speedtronic circular saw, in use here on several layers of waferboard.

Illus. 28. AEG cordless drill-driver, with Phillips driver bit chucked.

chuck is best. For heavier work, a professional model with a ½-inch chuck is good, and many such drills are small enough, though quite heavy, to use for lighter work as well.

For general woodworking, though, you do not need the extremely heavy drills.

Cordless drills are still not as common as standard electric drills, though, to be honest, I use my cordless more than my standard. Forget about saving money on cordless drills though, and if you want to use it as a screwdriver, buy a cordless screw-driver. Make sure your tool has a separate battery pack, and keep an extra energy pack on hand (this holds true for any cord-less tool). If you want a cordless drill, buy one listed as a professional model. The extra cost will be there, but is not extreme, and the durability over time is more than worth the difference (Illus. 28).

You may want to make sure you buy all your cordless tools in the same line to make certain battery packs are the same, thus assuring an extra supply of energy when they run low.

Reciprocating Saws. A reciprocating saw is one of those items you don't really see the need for until it becomes essential. Making pole joints is one example of a job not sufficiently covered by other power tools. Reciprocating saws offer almost as wide a blade choice as bayonet saws, and a good bit more power, with a heavier, sometimes longer blade (Illus. 29).

My preference is simple again. Two-speed models are slightly more powerful than the variable speed units, and the pro models are much better than any consumer models (if anyone still makes those). Cost variations here are truly minimal.

Illus. 29. Ryobi's two-speed reciprocating saw.

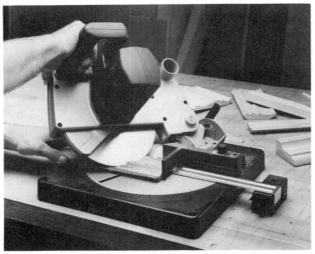

Illus. 30. Black & Decker's 8¼-inch-compound mitre saw. (Courtesy of Black & Decker.)

Power Mitre Saws Power mitre boxes may well be considered stationary tools, as they need a stand to provide the most accurate cuts, but they can also be operated on a board laid across sawhorses, or, in a pinch, on the ground (Illus. 30).

A small (about 8½-inch) saw has enough power for its rated capacities, but it has problems holding some angles over a long series of cuts. There is a certain amount of drift brought on by a light saw. Larger (10-inch or thereabout) saws can be near monsters (mine was 64 pounds in its box, and not much less unpacked). It runs best on a separate circuit unless you like dimming lights and will slice through, at 90°, a 2 by 6 or a 3 by 6—without pause. It also holds its settings (Illus. 31).

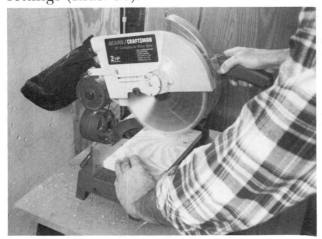

Illus. 31. Craftsman compound mitre saw.

Planer. Various tools, such as a planer, make practical the use of rough-sawn wood. Most (though not all) birdhouses are made with surfaced, or planed, woods, but having your own shop planer does make a difference.

At one time, only the most serious woodworker could afford a planer of any worth, but in recent years prices have taken a nose dive for decent quality tools. Purists might prefer big machines, but most of us need to remember we're not doing production-line planing (Illus. 32).

That's a quick roundup of the most important power tools for the projects in this book. I've made some comments I'm sure will make a few people happy, and a few unhappy, and that's fine, since my hope is those comments are of value to you.

Illus. 32. Ryobi's portable planer.

3
Hand Tools

Hand tools are traditional woodworking tools, those that use nothing more than our own muscle power to operate, that are truly capable of doing any of these projects if you're willing to spend the time and effort that working by hand requires. Hand tools also include measuring tools, most of which have yet to be electronically replaced, though such items as an electronic square are giving greater accuracy than ever before possible.

Most of your fastening work will be done with hand tools (hammers, screwdrivers, etc.). Some screwdriving can be carried out with power, but in really fine work, it is best to go with hand power—sensitivity is

Illus. 33. An array of hammers, saws, screwdrivers, chisels, clamps and other tools.

greater, especially when a screw is liable to split a piece of wood.

Handsaws

As do most other tools, handsaws come in a variety of styles, shapes, and designs to meet varied job requirements, and the variety has increased in recent years (Illus. 33).

Panel saws. For most projects in this book, two saws are helpful, the crosscut saw and the rip saw, and pinching a penny here means you'll probably mess up the work because the tool won't be as accurate as necessary. No matter what cutting you have to do, never buy anything less than a medium-grade handsaw and top-of-the-line is smarter.

As a basic, figure on an eight- to ten-tooth-per-inch crosscut saw, and six-tooth (or less)-per-inch ripsaw, and there's nothing wrong with keeping a variety. You can, if you wish, select a crosscut saw with a dozen teeth per inch, but that, while producing a smoother cut, requires more effort to use. I keep a wide selection of handsaws, even though my use of them is not as frequent as it once was—and probably not as frequent as it should be.

Coping saws. The coping saw is a scroll saw without the motor. Various versions are available, and I use two or three, from time to time, one with a deep neck to allow cut-

ting to the center of about a 12-inch board and the others for more routine work. All mine use standard 6⅜-inch blades. Fancier versions are available that will allow you to do precise work to the center of boards as much as 3 feet across (these are called marquetry saws and are meant for *very* fine work, usually on veneers).

Standard coping saws are pretty much limited to a foot-wide board, or a bit over 6 inches in frame height, but some have cast aluminum frame and allow cuts to 10 inches, thus making work to the center of an 18- or 20-inch board possible. These are slightly more costly, but the locked-to-the-frame handles won't turn with the cut, as many scroll saw handles do.

Hacksaws. Although mostly used on metals, hacksaws can cut any material with the appropriate blade. If you do much work with the plastic portions of the projects, you may find one handy, though except for the metal parts it is not truly essential because most handsaws and power saws will cut plastics (Illus. 34).

Hammers

Assembly tools par excellence, hammers have been with us so long their origins are shrouded in the mists of time (Illus. 35).

Claw hammers. The claw hammer is used to drive, and remove, nails (relatively small, bent nails use a crow bar or other appro-

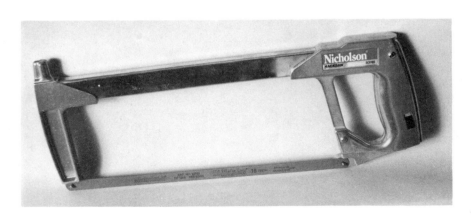

Illus. 34. Nicholson hacksaw.

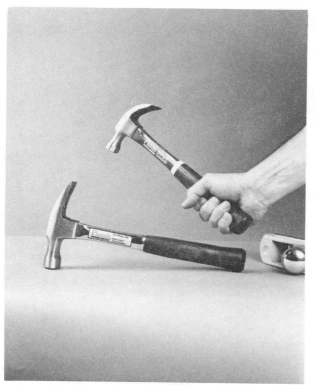
Illus. 35. Curved and straight claw hammers.

priate tool for jerking out large nails, unless you enjoy replacing hammer handles). Head weights may be critical in some uses, but for birdhouse and feeder projects, the fairly standard 16-ounce version will do quite well, as will the 13-ounce lightweight. Handle material is a matter of choice. I use all types and find a slight preference for wood and fibreglass over steel, but otherwise have no objections to using any. For the work done on these projects, I think you'll find a curved claw hammer gives a slightly better balance than does a straight, or rip, claw (Illus. 36).

Soft hammers. Soft hammers vary from rawhide heads, to rubber and plastic. Currently, I'm using several shot-loaded models, and find they work very well. One feature that I like is a slim-line head, and that hammer probably gets more inside work than any other when things have to be nudged into place, because its small head circumference makes it easy to get into tight spots.

Screwdrivers

Screwdrivers are items we all have more than a few of and seldom consider. Make sure though, you have one with a handle that fits your hand from a company you trust, and you've about covered the bases.

Tip styles must match the screwhead styles, of course, and need to be accurately cut. Better standard screwdrivers are machined after being formed, and will show slight machining marks.

Efficiency is the key to many of the newer screwhead styles. They grip the driver better, so they're more easily placed with power drivers, with less slippage.

Drills

For those times when no electric power of any kind is available, or likely to be, hand drills, bit braces, and push drills are invaluable. Bit braces with 10- or 12-inch swings are for holes ¼ inch or larger, and mine tends to get only those over ½ inch or so. Hand drills work, usually, with bits up to ⅜

Illus. 36. Fibreglass-handled curved-claw 16-ounce hammer, with folding rule and adjustable square.

Illus. 37. Stanley 10-inch bit brace and expansive kit—items useful for making holes up to about 3 inches in diameter.

inch, and push drills with even smaller bits. Most push drills carry their bits in the handle, and will not work with any other kind. They're ideal for drilling as an afterthought, when, for example, you've erected a birdhouse but forgotten to provide ventilation holes for it (Illus. 37).

Such hand tools may or may not have an overall value not supplied by power tools, but don't expect it to be in costs, since the power drills cost about the same in most areas (Illus. 38).

Measuring Tools

Measuring tools are your step to accuracy. While we could use a knotted length of cord to lay out everything we do in woodworking, or in many other crafts, modern measuring tools have developed over time to allow us to be a touch more precise than that (Illus. 39).

For the projects in this book, you'll need a folding rule (or 10-foot measuring tape), some type of square, a level, and a sliding

Illus. 38. Stanley hand drill.

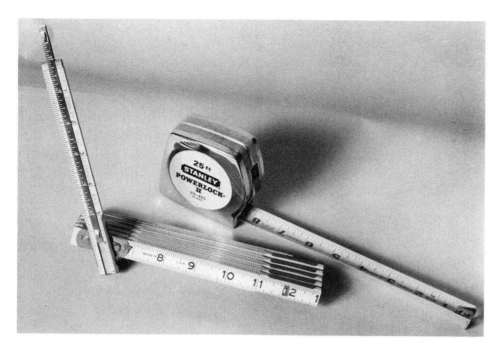

Illus 39. Primary measuring tools, a tape and a folding rule.

T-bevel, though this is pretty much optional (Illus. 40).

Folding rules. Folding rules are simply a series of boxwood or other light hardwood sticks, about ½ inch across, and 6 inches long, with brass hinges. They're marked in a variety of ways, depending on intended uses—mason's folding rules have different units than a carpenter's. Most are 6 feet long, some 8 feet. The best kinds have a yellow overall finish with black and red markings, and a 6-inch-long, brass sliding rule on one section for taking inside measurements (hole depths and such). Avoid metal folding rules, though fibreglass is acceptable. There is usually not much difference in price (Illus. 41).

Measuring tapes. Measuring tapes come in a number of lengths (Illus. 42), but for most birdhouse purposes, between 10 and 12 feet long is sufficient. Most measuring tapes are made of metal, ½ inch (for the shorter

Illus. 40. A solid square. Note the measuring tape in the photo being tilted slightly to get the markings closer to the point being marked as an aid to accuracy.

Hand Tools 31

Illus. 41. This array of Stanley and Lufkin tapes covers most needs.

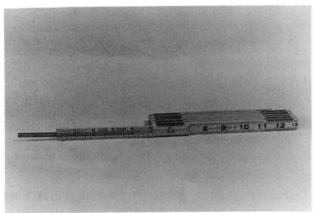

Illus. 42. Lufkin folding rule, with brass slip-out end.

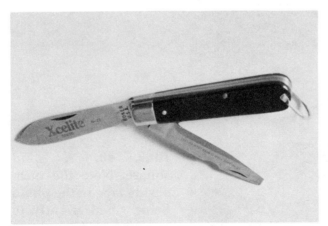

Illus. 43. Electrician's knife makes a good all-round marking, scraping, and cutting tool.

ones) to 1 inch wide. The shorter tapes are most useful because they're lighter and easier to handle on small projects, while the larger ones are great for larger jobs, but are bulky and heavy. Look for a good, solid case and a well-marked blade with a hooked end to catch over the workpiece.

Measuring tapes provide greatest marking accuracy if you tilt the slightly curled edges of the blade down to the surface to be marked. The same technique works with folding rules which are often nearly ¼ inch thick; Just tilt the rule down flush to the surface, and make your mark.

Squares. There is a variety of woodworking squares around today. Many are quite nice, most are cheap, and some are even accurate. When you select a square, remember how much the quality of your work depends on them.

As with any measuring and marking tool, look for clarity of marking, which in the case of squares might be contained in the depth of the cuts in the tongue, with or without pigment. Check to see that the handle and blade are securely fastened together (combination squares do not fasten together securely, because the handle slides on the blade, so that they are inherently less accurate than any solidly made square). If possible, use a small machinist's square to check the woodworking square for accuracy. Minor adjustments can be easily made by tapping the woodworking square on a chunk of wood to bring it into alignment. For most project work, a well made 12-inch square, or even an 8-inch one, is sufficient.

Levels. For the purposes of erecting pole mounted birdhouses and feeders, you'll need some kind of level to plumb the pole. Depending on your other uses for the level, you could get a 9-inch or 2-foot level. Neither is that expensive.

Measuring tools also include items for making marks on your workpieces. Either a scratch awl or a carpenter's pencil will put you in good shape. The carpenter's pencil differs from a basic pencil in that it is flat and sharpened with a penknife. The point can be made as sharp as required and doesn't break as easily as does a standard round point. Knives can be used to mark in place of awls. A basic pocketknife, or a utility knife will serve you well (Illus. 43).

Mitre Boxes

The variety of nonpowered mitre boxes, like the variety of powered mitre boxes, has increased greatly in recent years, which is good for us as well as for the manufacturers.

Styles vary. Some mitre boxes can mitre well, but cannot make compound cuts; others can (mostly top-of-the-line models). Make sure, though, that it has a right angle capacity of about 9½ inches or more. It's also nice to be able to set depth stops to cut dadoes, and have major angles pre-set (Illus. 44).

A less expensive alternative is simple saw guides matched with a good panel saw for almost all the mitre cuts you will need to make.

Planes

All my planes are cast iron, except for two wood-bodied planes. The small general plane is superb, as is the even smaller block plane, but in most cases, I go with the metal planes (Illus. 45).

Planes require some tune-up before they are used, though most top models are impressively finished. At the least, all the plane irons will need a good honing and deburring before use, and you'll almost certainly find it pays to disassemble them and check all fittings for flatness (soles, in particularly) and general fit. True them up as you reassemble them (Illus. 46).

Generally, you may find a need for a small, low-angle block plane to cut end grain, and for a 9-inch jack or bench plane for more general squaring-up of boards (Illus. 47).

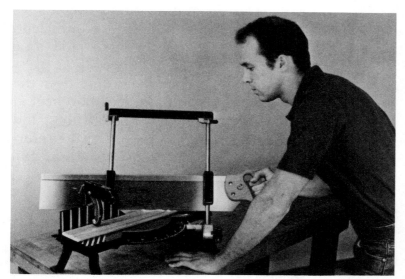

Illus. 44. Craftsman mitre box, with 10-inch capacity at 90°. (Courtesy of Sears, Roebuck & Co.)

Illus. 45. Stanley bench and low-angle block planes.

Illus. 46. (right) E.C.E. bench plane.

Illus. 47. (below) E.C.E. high-angle block plane.

Chisels

Chisels are almost essential for cutting mortises, and for most uses, a relatively cheap set in ¼- and ½- and ¾-inch sizes that you tune up and de-burr is sufficient. A Japanese 1200 grit (or less) waterstone does the best job.

Various tests run by magazines over the years have indicated little difference in blade metals in chisels between the best and the cheapest, and I have no real preferences among my different sets (Illus. 48).

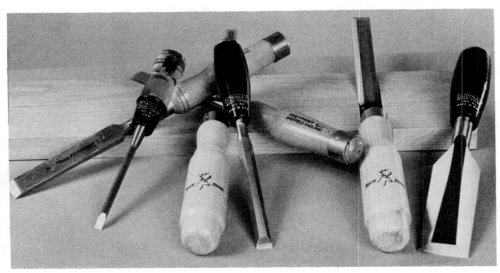

Illus. 48. A part of the chisel selection I keep on hand.

4
Jigs and Aids

One of the fascinating aspects of woodworking is that virtually every tool's limitations disappear with the aid of a few simple devices (Illus. 49).

The array of commercial devices on the market isn't nearly as great as the number of readily available plans for homebuilt woodworking jigs and devices, but some commercial units are easier to install and simpler to use than homemade jigs: the AccuJoint and the Shophelper are cases in point. While there are a number of plans out there for finger joint jigs, I've always had trouble constructing them and getting

Illus. 49. Black & Decker's Workmate 400 is probably the best all-round portable jig and shop aid available. (Courtesy of Black & Decker.)

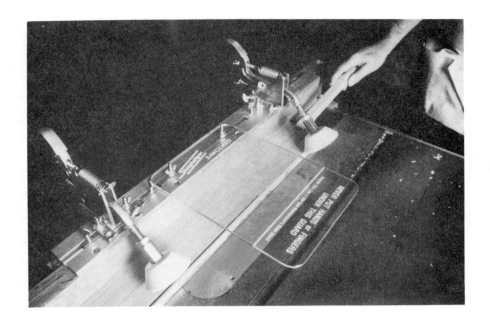

Illus. 50. The Shophelper doing its stuff.

them to work *consistently*. The AccuJoint, like almost all commercial set-ups, requires a few wooden bits and pieces and an hour or two of time to get working correctly, but finger joints become simple and quick. The Shophelper (Illus. 50–51), while not on the jig list, can be an invaluable aid with rip cuts.

Another nice thing about the Shophelper is it lets me photograph rip cuts with no worries about a saw guard blocking the shots, and far fewer worries about getting hit with flying wood, or losing a finger, neither of which results I would expect to find thrilling.

The Shophelper protects and helps (and it is definitely a worthwhile help when making rips in longer boards, especially in long and narrow stock) during rip cuts; but to date, I've found no such device that is as worthwhile, and as easily added or removed, for crosscuts. Keep in mind, though, that with shipping and bits and pieces either on hand or bought, we're looking at a considerable price for a complete unit—and there are a couple of accessories I did NOT buy.

The Shophelper's castings are aluminum, with good, heavy steel threaded bolts and

Illus. 51. The Shophelper makes longer cuts easier.

nuts, and very heavy springs. The blade guard is heavy plastic and may be a polycarbonate such as Lexan for its weight and appearance. The metal castings are reasonably clean, but the metal itself is unfinished; thus, it's a little scarred-looking and dull.

The mostly plastic AccuJoint has red plastic guides, and, again, metal pieces that are fairly rough in finish, but not as visible. The one wood section appears to be maple. Overall cost here is much lower than the Shophelper, so finish should possibly be less of a complaint.

The AccuJoint is an indexing jig for finger joints in four sizes, ⅛, ¼, ⅜, and ½ inch. After you get the guide board cut for the basic set-up, it becomes very simple to use. You'll need good vertical drilling to place the tiny metal dowel pin—my only real objection to the guide is the fact that these tiny dowels are certain to be easily and quickly lost (two are provided). The basic guide is aluminum, and three plastic accessory guides are provided. Use the basic guide for ⅛-inch finger joints. Mount a guide board extending an equal distance on each side of the saw blade on the mitre gauge. Clamp the board to be cut in the AccuJoint, after an initial cut for depth is made in the guide board with the dado head set at the proper width. Hold the clamped board and jig firmly against the mitre gauge board, and drill the hole for the dowel, after which the initial cut is made. Move the guide a slot at a time onto the guide pin or dowel; the finger joints are then rapidly and accurately cut. This not only eases the job of accurate finger joint production, it cuts out the need to produce a complex and necessarily finicky home guide.

Finger joints have been described as *the* strongest joints in woodworking, mostly by people who should know better. It does provide a huge glue area, and thus is quite strong, but not stronger than either dovetails in drawers or mortise-and-tenon joints in their appropriate places. It is a handy joint, relatively easy and quick to cut with the proper jigs, and quite attractive when properly done. It is not the strongest joint in woodworking.

Router Jigs

Router jigs, in my mind, are edge guides to hold you on a straight or appropriately curved line. My most common jig use, though, is when I'll need to groove or otherwise use a bit at an angle not provided for by a face on the board, or the simple circle and straight line guides. In those cases, I place the requisite guides in place with short bar clamps or C-clamps (spring clamps will do when the rise of the clamp gets in the way). This works well for angled cuts, stops, and so on.

Beyond that, standard dovetail guides are about the only router jigs I've ever required (except lettering templates).

Table Saw Jigs

Mitring on a table saw can be a chancy operation; cuts at an angle other than 90° can be dangerous, and you're more likely to waste stock and time trying to hold everything in place and get a clean, accurate cut. Some years ago, I discovered a version of a sliding mitre table that makes a fine difference. To give credit where credit is due, the table is from *Power Tool Woodworking for Everyone*, by R. J. DeCristoforo and published by Shopsmith, Inc. It contains an incredible amount of valuable detail.

To build the sliding mitre table, you need a 20 x 25-inch section of plastic-laminate-covered particle board. Use the laminate face down—it lessens friction between sliding table and stationary table. Use strips of maple, ash or oak to make 20-inch-long strips to fit both mitre gauge slots in your table saw table. Measure your grooves individually, and make sure you're as accurate as possible. Attach the strips with brass wood screws (#6 x ¾ inch) every 3 inches. Now, you need to cut two hardwood fence sections, 1¼ x 2¼ x 17 inches.

Mitre the ends that meet and run a saw kerf between the mitred boards after they're attached to the sliding table. (Use countersunk flathead brass wood screws again, this time #8 x 1¾ inch, and a good carpenter's glue as well: attach one fence section, let the glue dry, and then use an accurate carpenter's or machinist's square to place the second fence.) Line the forward faces of both fences with fine grit sandpaper, glued in place. The mitre fences mount 7½ inches back from the front edge of the sliding table, and the saw kerf is 12½ inches in from the left-hand edge. This jig works best if you always cut matching mitres with it; that is, cut the first piece on the left side, and the next piece on the right side—or vice versa—so that they mate at that corner.

As with all jigs, the more care you put into getting things accurate, the more accurate results you'll get. Maintaining the jig and proper finishing is also going to help keep it accurate for a long period of time. I sanded mine carefully with 220-grit paper, finish-sealed it, laid on a second coat of tung oil (undiluted this time) and waxed the laminate and the maple guides heavily with paste floor wax, the same wax I use on my saw tables, when the tung oil dried. I used that unit for some time, before it wore out. I've just completed a new one, and expect to use it even longer.

Taper jigs are part and parcel of working rips on a table saw, and over the years I got fed up with trying to make a decent one that no one would mistake for something else and use for kindling. I finally picked up a relatively cheap commercial device (called, oddly enough, Taper Jig) that produces tapers up to 15° or 3 inches per foot. It works well and easily, and can be used, depending on how you mount the hardware, to either side of the blade. I have a tendency to use it on the left side of the blade, with the counterclockwise Shop-helper in place, keeping my body well to the left of *anything* that might go wrong. "Super Chicken" works alone most of the

time, and is not about to get hurt living ten miles from the nearest hospital.

For our purposes a cutoff jig is the only other table saw jig you'll need. Cutoff jigs follow a simple rule: under no circumstances are both mitre gauge and rip fence to be used at the same time on a table saw. Use clamps to place cutoff jig blocks for use with the mitre gauge, and make sure the blocks end just before the workpiece makes contact with the saw blade (at least). This way, you can use it as a guide, without the jig binding the work and the saw trying to fling it back at you. The safest course is to make sure that by the time the workpiece has started to touch the saw blade, it is entirely free of the guide, thus virtually eliminating any chance of binding.

Many people use the rip fence as a part of the cutoff jig set-up. This is safe *if* you clamp an auxiliary fence to the rip fence, so that it ends as mentioned above for the jig. *There must not be follow-up contact by the jig or the rip fence on the pieces after they have contacted the saw blade!*

Larger panels and longer boards require some adaptations, and one in particular is handy for producing units of the same size. To cut (for example) a 2 x 4-foot panel into six 3-inch-wide x 2-foot-long boards, set the rip fence to give a single 3-inch-wide cut from a scribed (with pencil, not an awl) mark along the back of the rip fence and cut the first piece. Loosen the rip fence, move it, place the cutoff piece between rip fence and scribed mark, and lock the rip fence. Make the second cut. Keep repeating the procedure, adding pieces between fence and mark until all cuts are made.

Other techniques help in various situations. Always, for example, glue fine sandpaper on the mitre gauge face: if you use an auxiliary face on the mitre gauge, you can increase the bearing and holding surfaces and get a great increase in gripping strength.

An auxiliary fence on the rip fence is always a good idea. The auxiliary fence should be a dense-grained hardwood such as maple, which should then be waxed (paste floor wax works best).

Some Final Hints

Table saws should always have their tables coated with paste floor wax, with repeat coatings every six to ten hours of use to maintain the slick surface (for best slipperiness, coat and buff the table at least three times when new). You may have to use alcohol or other solvent to get the factory-applied grease off the table surface. Apply the same coating to the rip fence guide rails to aid movement (though some mechanisms are more prone to slippage in use with this treatment, so use a bit of common sense: if your rip fence doesn't have a good positive lock do not coat it with wax to decrease friction).

Well maintained saw blades are vital to accurate cutting. It really doesn't take long, particularly with pitch-filled woods such as pine and cedar, to load a saw blade with gum. Pop the blade off, lay it on about six layers of newspaper and spray it with a good grade of oven cleaner. Wipe off, let it dry, and coat the blade—very lightly—with a dry lubricant to prevent rust. Be careful, lubrication can be touchy. It is a toss-up as to which causes more problems: rust on the blade, or lubricant on the first few cuts of wood. Simplify matters and run some scrap wood cuts through a freshly lubricated blade.

Saw blades require more attention than we give them (though probably less than the saw blade makers say they need). Use the best blade for each purpose you can afford; whether it's carbide-tipped or not, keep it clean and sharp, and things will usually go well. Don't be afraid to talk to friends and local crafts men and women to see what their preferences are. If possible, try out different brands of the more costly blades before making your selection. There's a lot of difference between being unhappy with a $15 saw blade and being unhappy with a $90 one, and either price is quite easy to find these days (Illus. 52–55).

Illus. 52. Craftsman tenoning jig.

Illus. 53. Cutoff jig.

Illus. 54. Mitre gauge board clamp is great for preventing board creep during crosscuts.

Illus. 55. Some form of push stick is essential for tight rip cuts. This one is from Shopsmith.

5
Birds and Their Appetites

There is a wide variety of birds you might see in specific areas of this country, some more likely than others. Since we're considering backyard nests and feeders, here's some of the most common visitors you'll encounter.

Your Visitors

Cardinal. Cardinals are beautiful birds with a preference for dense shrubbery, particularly shrubs that produce berries and fruits. Feed preferences are sunflower seeds, scratch feeds, and cracked corn. In most areas of the eastern United States they do not migrate, so feeding will keep them in your garden all winter.

Bluebird. Bluebirds were once disappearing because their nesting areas were getting wiped out, but in recent years bluebird nesting boxes, with entry holes cut no larger than 1½ inches (to keep out unwanted guests), has helped increase their numbers. Bluebirds stick pretty much to the eastern United States and do not migrate, while also showing a marked preference for shrubs that have winter fruits, berries and seeds.

Blue jay. You can get a mixed bag of emotions on the value of having blue jays come to a feeder. They are attractive and will eat just about any seed you put out, though they have a marked preference for sunflower seeds. Their migration is just a nim-ble-winged hop over or down to a milder clime, and they remain on the scene in most of eastern North America all winter.

Junco. The junco is a small, jittery bird, and a ground feeder. Winter sees them scattered throughout the country, but in other seasons they're oriented to Canada and the northeast and northwest United States. They'll eat crumbs, but are best served with sunflower seeds, suet and other high-energy foods. Juncos like shrubbery, both as a windbreak and a place to hide from predators.

Goldfinch. This bright little bird is a worker, with a preference for picking its own seeds from sunflower shells. Goldfinches build compact nests in small trees and woody shrubs over much of the United States and southern Canada. They usually winter in the Midwest and South. A standard wild-seed mix will draw them to a feeder.

Grosbeak. Although in some parts of the United States seeing an evening grosbeak is a rare experience, they dominated my feeders when I lived in upstate New York. They love to eat sunflower seeds, and like shade trees and low shrubbery.

Bushtit. The bushtit is a western bird, spending time in Washington, Oregon, California, and other southwestern states. It has no use for a woodworker's contribution to housing, but will visit your feeder to collect corn, suet, and peanut butter.

Chickadee. The chickadee is a personal favorite, probably because it is the only species I've managed to hand-feed in the wild. This is the garden bird least fearful of humans, and they love sunflower seeds, even though they appear too small to crack them (the work evidently causes few problems, because they'll eat bags of the seeds). They also like suet, bread crumbs and peanut butter. Small and mostly grey, chickadees are found throughout most of southern Canada and the northern United States on a year-round basis. They migrate as far south as North Carolina, but will still use birdhouses in winter, and as a group will get together in a house, evidently to keep warm.

Finch. Finches tend to stay close to people, but they also will flock around fruit and berry-bearing plants. Finches will use birdhouses and feed on sunflower seeds, millet, bread crumbs, and fruit bits, and seem willing to try other seeds. They are voracious eaters, even for birds. They're found year-round throughout most of the West, southern New England, and eastern New York.

Flicker. This large bird is a member of the woodpecker family and likes insects for dinner. Its bill is more curved than a woodpecker's, and thus is better suited to feeding in insect nests than in trees. Flickers travel in flocks, and can be found pretty much throughout the United States year-round, and in Canada during the summer. Rough-wood birdhouses suit them best, as do suet and peanut butter for a diet.

Nuthatch. Nuthatches are about the same size as sparrows. They can be found throughout the United States. This bird grips tree trunks and other such spots quite well, and can be found checking you out from a position that seems dizzyingly close to upside down. Their tastes are wide ranging, and includes sunflower seeds, pump-

kin seeds, peanut butter, breads and sweet cakes, as well as suet.

Martin. Purple martins are widely known as the best insect catchers around, and pretty well live up to their reputation. They nest in groups—the reason martin houses are apartment style—and a single house may see as many as thirty nesting *pairs*. Martin houses are best erected after the martins arrive in the spring so pest birds like starlings won't take advantage of the large entry holes, thus forcing the more desirable martins to move on. Martins nest over most of the eastern United States well into southern Canada during the summer, and also may be found along the Pacific coast. These are truly migratory birds, so you won't see them feeding in the winter.

Oriole. The oriole is a black and orange bird that nests high, and both the Baltimore oriole in the East and the Bullock oriole in the West are migratory. These birds would most love a materials box that contains some soft yarn threads for their nests, but if any are around late in the year, they'll feed on suet, berries, and leftover fruit.

Robin. Robins are abundant in Canada and the United States, and are usually migratory—the first signs of spring. However, they've been known to spend the entire year in some parts of the United States and British Columbia. Robins like fruit in feeders, and nest in open shelves rather than in closed birdhouses.

Barn swallow. This forked-tail swallow is probably the most colorful, with an orange front and deep blue back. It is also the only member of the swallow family outside the purple martin likely to nest in or around a garden or yard. Barn swallows feed almost exclusively on insects so, added to their migratory habits, you probably won't attract them to a winter feeder, but suet may bring them around. Swallows prefer high open nesting shelves.

Tufted titmouse. These are small birds, found in most parts of the eastern United

States on a year-round basis. Titmice feed on sunflower seeds, suet, rice, raisins, bread, and other seeds during winter, and nest in birdhouses, especially rough-finished wood models.

Towhee. Rufous-sided towhees are easy to identify, but often hard to spot. If you note a black and white bird with reddish brown sides, you've got one. Towhees like messy yards—a specialty of mine—and berry bushes, bread crumbs, and most seeds. The towhees are year-round birds in the western and southern United States, and spend the summer as far north as southern Canada.

Woodpecker. Over the years, I've managed to spot a number of woodpeckers, including some fairly rare ones, and the downy woodpecker is the most common one in the United States and Canada. Rustic birdhouses, made of bark-on or rough-sawn wood, are fine with them, though they do prefer a sawdust floor. Downies like suet, bread crumbs, berries, cherries, and they also eat seeds. The red-headed woodpecker is fairly common in the southeast and parts of the midwest United States. The head is entirely red while the black wings have large white patches. They prefer plains, fields, and open deciduous forest. Red-headed woodpeckers are often attracted to gardens surrounded by large trees, and it will use a nesting box mounted high on a tree in the open. The red-bellied woodpecker is nonmigratory, and so is likely to be a winter visitor. Both these birds like wild and cultivated fruits and berries, and will visit a feeder for suet, sunflower seeds, cracked corn, and some baked goods. The red-bellied woodpecker will also use man-made birdhouses.

Wren. Wrens love gardens, and house wrens will live in almost anything. They'll eat a lot of insects, and will also munch any suet that's out. They live in most parts of the United States and Canada.

Although I didn't mention them, don't be surprised to see sapsuckers, owls, vireos, tanagers, pine siskins, thrushes, palm warblers, waxwings, doves, sparrows, phoebes, humming birds, and brown creepers, to mention just a few. The point is, there are a lot of birds out there that may do better with our help, and that may add to our lives through their colorful feathers and bright chirpy behavior.

Bird Feeds

When you're ready to feed the birds, remember three things. The first is that the most attractive bird feeders in the world will not help at all without the right food. The birds you lure directly depends on the feed you lay out. The second thing to remember is you're going to attract a lot of birds you wish would stay away. There's no help for that, because there's simply too much crossover of food needs and tastes to allow for perfect selection.

The third, and most important thing to remember is: do *not* start feeding birds as winter approaches unless you intend, and are able, to keep feeding them throughout the cold months. Birds that might go elsewhere to eat, or simply migrate, may stay in the area of your feeder, and if the food is suddenly cut off when there is no reasonable alternative supply—as there would be during the growing months—there is every possibility those extra birds could starve to death. There's no great harm, however, in stopping your feeding during those months when everything is up and growing. Many bird lovers break off feeding during spring, summer and early fall.

Most birds we attempt to feed are seed-eaters, though a number of insectivorous avians will come to seed and suet feeders. Since more people are now feeding birds, selling birdseed has become big business. *Wildbird* magazine contains many ads and listings for feeders, houses, and feeds, though I cannot honestly say the thought of spending nearly as much per pound for treated suet as I do for sirloin does much for me.

The best spots to buy birdseed are still rural supply shops especially if you buy amounts of twenty-five pounds and up, something I recommend for anyone serious about bird feeding. Most grocery stores offer good birdseed in several varieties, but they tend to come in small three and five pound bags and cost three to five times what you're apt to pay in feed shops. A better alternative is birding groups that supply feed at or near their cost (mostly because they order in bulk).

Sunflower seed. Sunflower seed isn't the most expensive or the bulkiest of bird feeds, but it can seem both at times, because an unshelled fifty pounds of seed takes a good-sized sack. Shelled sacks are lighter, but quite a bit more costly. Mixed birdseed comes with a fair amount of sunflower seed, either shelled or unshelled, slipped in, but because it is more expensive than other types of seed, gross amounts are still probably under ten percent.

Unshelled sunflower seed is a mixed blessing: Chickadees and nuthatches are willing to do the work, while starlings and sparrows, somewhat less desirable feeder visitors, do not like the work. Evening grosbeaks love sunflower seeds in any shape or form, and can be as big feeder hogs as starlings. The mixed part of the unshelled sunflower seed blessing comes with the mess that results. The shells end up thickly piled

Illus. 56. Thistle seed feeder, with a small pile of the tiny seeds.

under and around the feeders and, for some reason, they do not help plant growth, so you've got to rake it up.

Corn. Cracked corn is a great treat for many birds, and is reasonable in cost unless you buy it at a pet shop or grocery store. The larger the amount, the cheaper the corn, though prices vary.

Corn has a few problems. It shouldn't be fed whole, so you either have to crack it or pay to buy it cracked. Corn also spoils fairly quickly when wetted down by rain and subjected to mild weather (above freezing), so any remnants should be scraped or brushed away fairly quickly. Corn will attract almost the full array of feeder birds, including woodpeckers and songbirds.

Thistle. Thistle is the most costly of seeds per pound, in part because it bulks so little. You won't want to put out a lot, or waste what you do put out, so in the projects you'll find a special thistle feeder (Illus. 56). If thistle is bought in bulk through a club, the price is still high, but about half the price per pound. It'll draw finches, sparrows, chickadees, towhees, juncos and doves, among other birds.

Other grains. The different seeds that we supply birds with these days are mostly cereal grains. These are commonly grown, reasonably priced, and nutritious. Millet is a tiny round seed that makes up the bulk of many commercial birdseeds, with nearly four times the total food energy (calories) as raw corn. Milo (or sorghum) is a slightly larger seed, still round, with about the same food energy as millet or oats. Wheat, including buckwheat, offers just a shade less food energy than the oats and millet. Durum presents the highest caloric value of the wheats.

Illus. 57. Pouring mixed feed onto a flying wing ground feeder.

Scratch feed and grit. Birds do not have quite the same digestive system humans have; so, to allow them to digest their seeds, their digestive tract uses sand, shells or other small bits of grit to further the work of reducing edible seeds to digestible food. So, while it's neither a seed nor a feed, you cannot cause a bird any problems by scattering a handful of sand or broken eggshells in and around your feeders each week. Strange as it may seem, this could be essential to a bird's proper digestion.

Suet. Insectivorous birds require fatty foods to keep body energy high and suet is fat, pure and simple. It's trimmed from meats before they're slipped onto grocery shop shelves, and many supermarkets even package suet for sale in the winter. Put the suet out only in very cold weather, since few, if any, seed-preferring birds seem to need the extra energy in warmer weather, and suet spoils quickly.

You could also put out cakes, breads, peanut butter, peanuts, and various scraps of fruit and berries. Keep in mind, though, that cakes and breads as less desirable foods (especially in winter), because their nutritional values are lower. Birds are like children. They show a preference for sweets and easy things, but can easily mess up their nutritional needs by overfilling on junk food.

Mixing your own feed is not only fun, but a good way to save some money, if you have the cash to buy and the room to store several large sacks of the seeds you wish to use. As a start, try a mixture of half millet, twenty percent oats, and the rest unshelled sunflower seeds. Experiment over time to see what mixes draw what birds (Illus. 57).

Watching separate feeders is a good way to find out the preferences of our feathered friends. Select your seeds, place the feeders in a circle—at least thirty feet in diameter—and put one type of seed in each; then spend a couple of enjoyable hours checking to see what birds go to, and remain at, which feeders.

6
Birdhouse Designs

Simple A-Frame

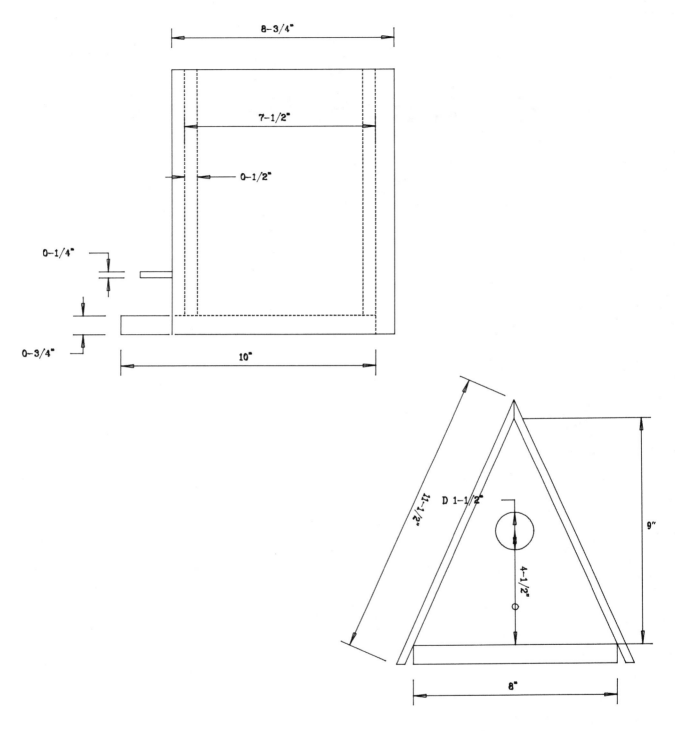

Illus. 58. Simple A-Frame. This doesn't need much in the way of directions. The roof fits together, of ½-inch stock, and is screwed, using #6 x 1¼-inch brass round-head wood screws, to the base. The base is ¾-inch thick, while the remainder is ½ inch. If desired, install a brace block inside the roof ridge, and use the house as a hanging model.

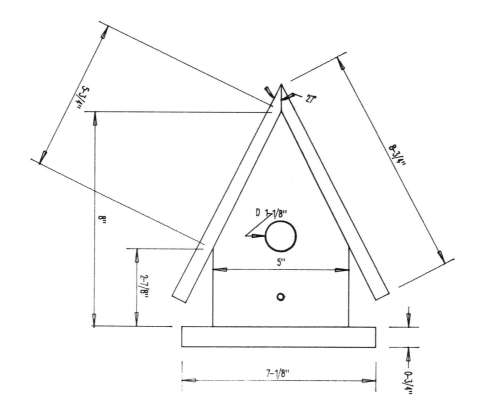

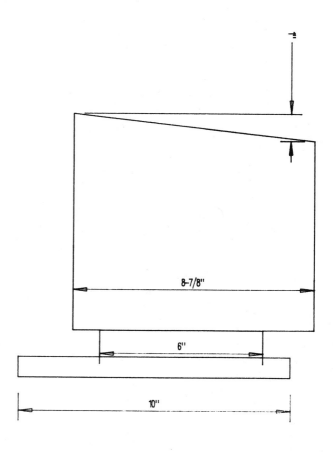

Illus. 59. A-Frame. Any material may be used, but for best results, redwood or cedar is recommended. Use ½-inch (finished size) stock for all but the floor. The house mounts on a pole from the floor, and two #6 x 1½-inch round-head screws will hold it in place on the floor.

This design can be adjusted to suit most birds. All joints are butts, and the only close to complex cut is the mitred and tapered roof-ridge line. This could be eliminated, making back and front identical except for holes, and making the design suitable for production runs.

Nesting Box

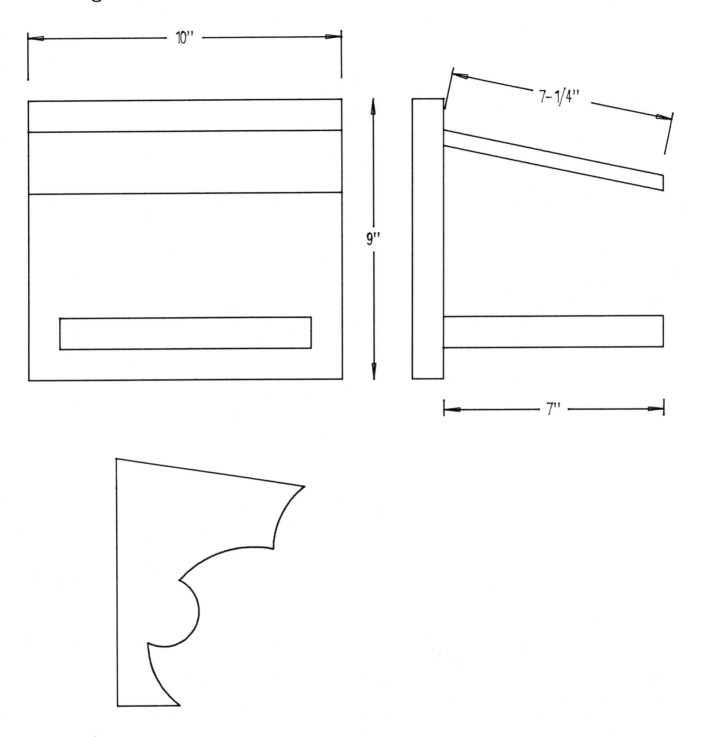

Illus. 60. Nesting Box. This simple box is ¾-inch or 1-inch material, and serves for those birds, such as robins, that prefer to nest with at least two sides open.

You can add a windbreak side using the enclosed pattern, or make up a pattern of your own.

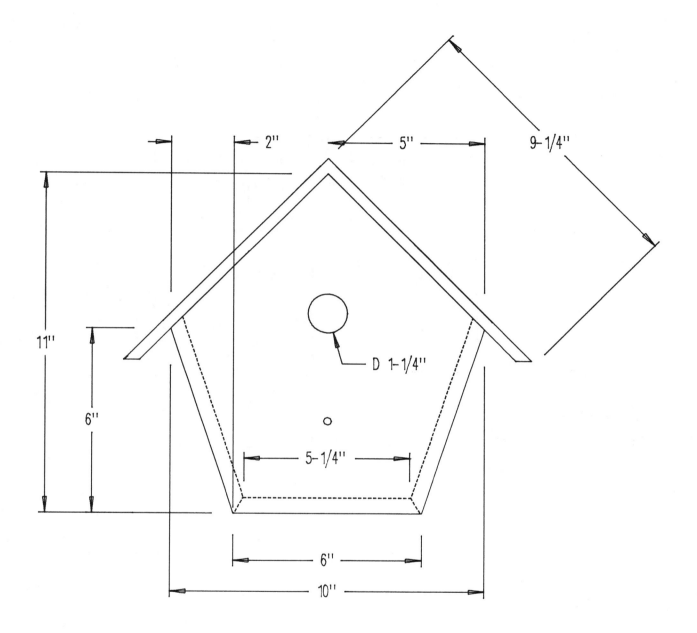

Illus. 61. Titmouse House. This house is designed with lighter ½-inch wood but can be adapted to ¾-inch wood. It is simple, with the sides 6-inches deep, and the roof overhanging 2 inches at the front and 1 inch at the rear, for a total length of 10 inches.

The house is best used in a hanging position, but adapts readily to pole mounting.

Flycatcher House

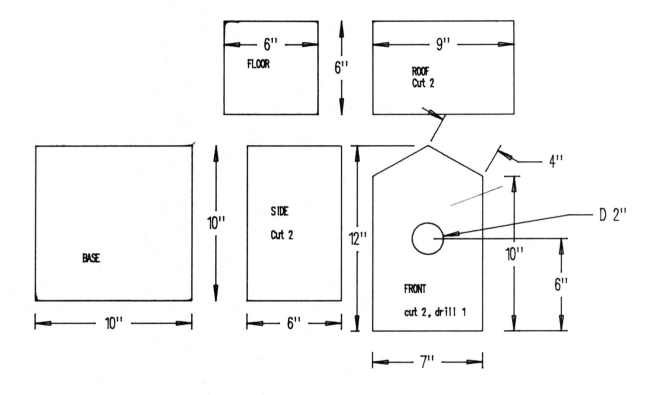

Illus. 62. Flycatcher House. Made entirely of ½-inch wood, this house inexpensively uses cedar or redwood, with shakes (trimmed cedar shim stock) used for the roof. Assemble with butt joints and use a plug for the floor insert with two wood screws (#6 or #4, 1-inch) holding the base on. Leave the eave lines on the side square. Cut to allow air in.

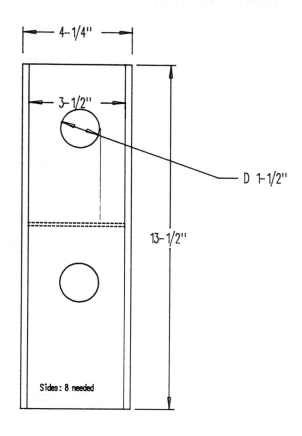

Octagonal Birdhouse

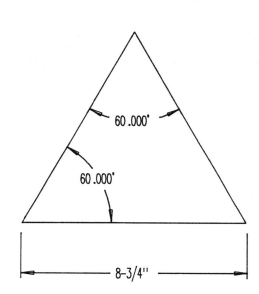

Illus. 63. Octagonal Birdhouse. This is designed to accept four nests, and its capacity can be doubled with a doubling in height.

The base is 8-inches across, and the second floor is 1½-inches less across (6½-inches), though all angles are identical. Make the second floor exactly like the base, except for its width. If you decide to raise the roof to 27 inches, make the resulting two extra floors the same size as the second floor.

The included angle for the octagons is 45°. That means, simply, that you need each cut to measure 22½° to mate correctly. Thus there are two long rips on each side of the wides, with the angle set at 22½°. The excluded angle there is 67½°.

For the base, and succeeding floors, make the cuts 45°, so the excluded angle is 135° .

The roof square is 8 inches on a side. It fits on top, directly under the roof triangles. The roof triangles require compound cuts. The 60° angle of the triangle brings the peaks together, while a rip of 45° is required for the side fit.

Attach the top with 1½-inch aluminum or brass nails near each corner. Use pilot holes to prevent splitting.

Birdhouse Designs 53

Assembled
Martin House

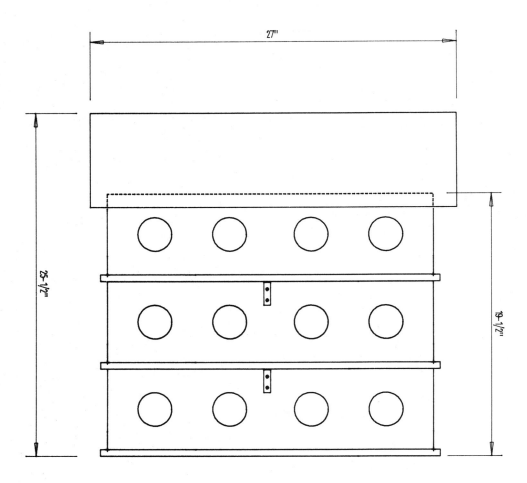

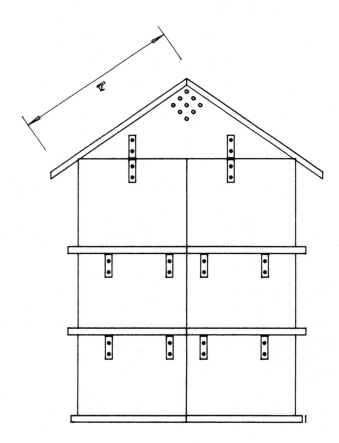

Illus. 64. Assembled Martin House. Martins like a decent amount of height for their nests, so you may wish to use a jointed pole to allow easy erection and cleaning of the house.

This house is large and moderately heavy. It is designed *only* for pole mounting, and requires a minimum of 2 x 4 cross bracing, half-lapped, under the floor for maximum security on the pole.

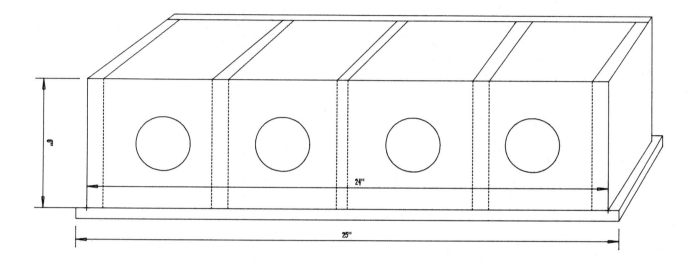

Illus. 65. Martin House Section. Attach this unit to others built in the same way to form several story high houses for Purple Martins. Use ¾-inch stock.

The house can be two-sided as well as multi-storied, simply by increasing the width of the base, adding three of the four second side parts, and using the back as a divider. (Drill four more entry holes, of course.) As it stands, the side width is 8 inches. Attach the units to each other by brass corner braces. These braces accept 2 small wood screws on each leg, and are readily available at hardware stores.

The braces used here are Stanley Hardware CD5351 1½ x 1½ inch Classic Brassware, which, quite literally, any hardware dealer can order.

Chickadee House with Variations

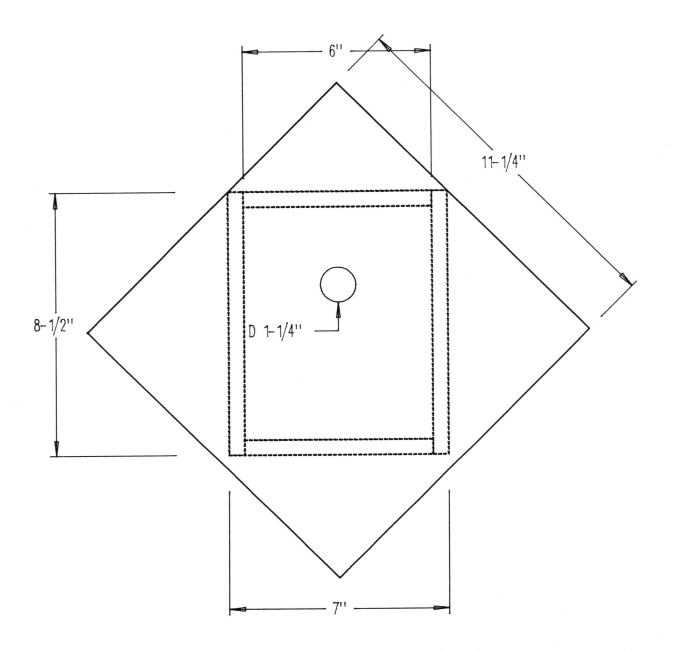

Illus. 66. Chickadee House. This simple house allows for all sorts of variations in the front and the back.

Shown here is a simple diamond, really nothing more than a square section of 1 x 12-inch lumber, nailed or screwed to the basic chickadee box.

The sides are 6 inches deep, as are the top and the bottom. It is designed for hanging.

You could try a circular piece, or a square of similar size or greater size with patterns cut in the edges.

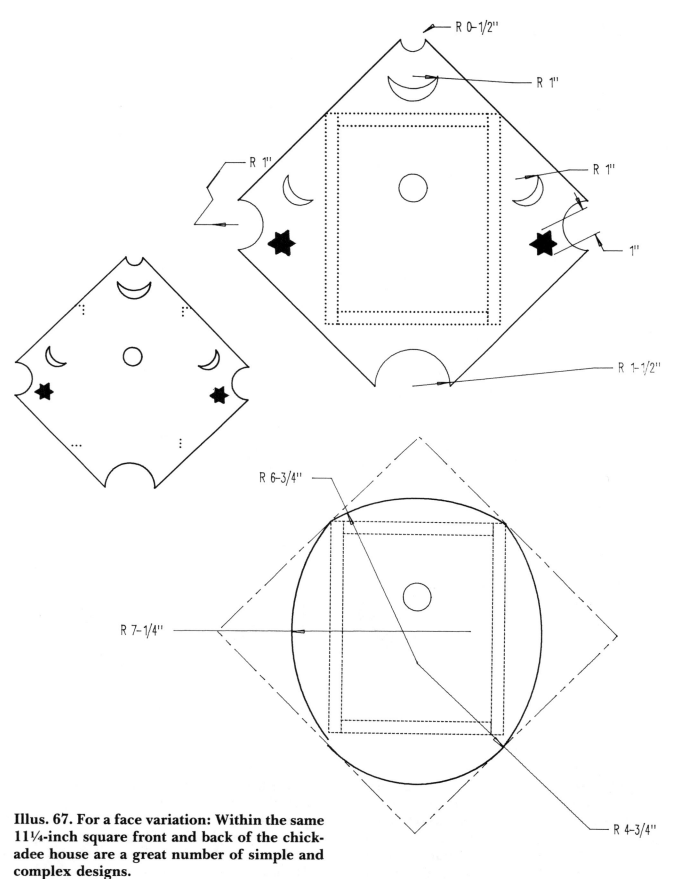

Illus. 67. For a face variation: Within the same 11¼-inch square front and back of the chickadee house are a great number of simple and complex designs.

The front pattern will also fit well within the standard 11¼-inch section.

Crazy Roof Birdhouse

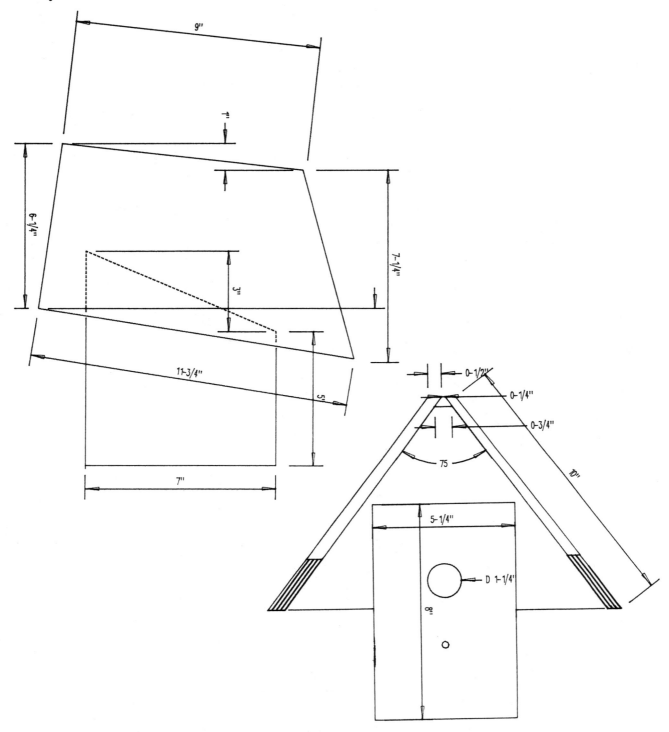

Illus. 68. Crazy Roof Birdhouse. This birdhouse is made of colorful woods (redwood or cedar), preferably not all heartwood. Using sapwood cuts durability, but adds to attractiveness with wildly varying grain patterns.

The overall size of the house makes it suitable for a number of birds, with only a mild change here and there—the depth and the size of the entry hole being the most important.

I would suggest that once you cut the basic pieces, fit them as you make trim cuts and work on the roof spline. The roof spline taper should remain the same from end to end.

The bottom is a butt-joint slip-in fit, held in place with three wood screws, one at the front, and one in each side. Butt-joint the sides.

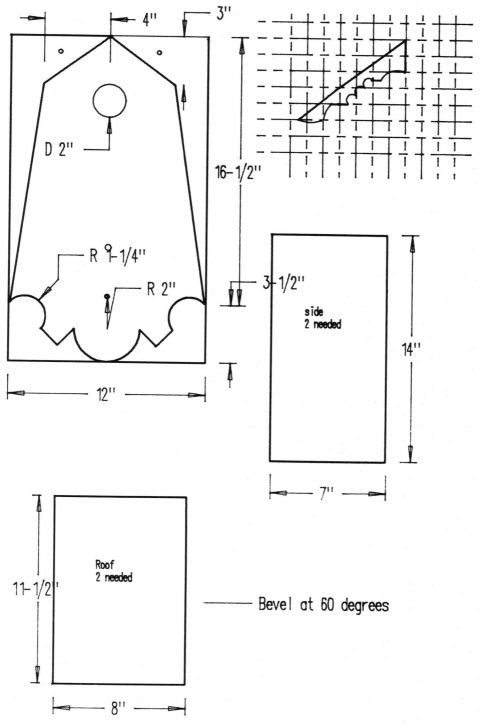

Flicker House

D 2"

16-1/2"

R 1-1/4"

R 2"

12"

3-1/2"

side
2 needed

14"

7"

4"

3"

Roof
2 needed

11-1/2"

8"

Bevel at 60 degrees

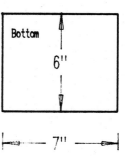

Bottom

6"

7"

Illus. 69. Flicker House. This design is simpler than it looks: the fancy scrollwork can be cut on a scroll saw—or it can be left off, and the front simply assembled on the sides. Alternatively, you could add in the angle cuts on the front, and leave off the scrollwork. Use butt joints and small nails (1¼ inch) for assembly.

Swing-Front Flicker House

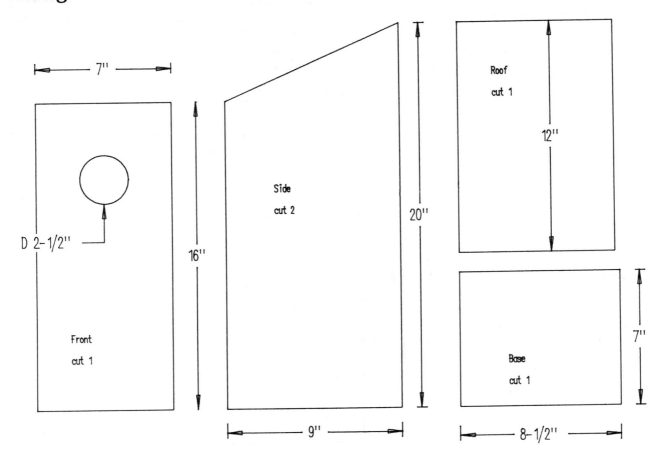

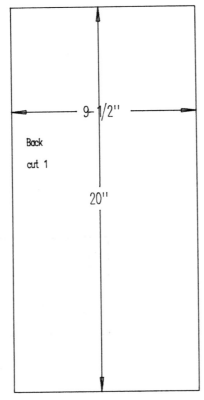

Illus. 70. Swing-Front Flicker House. Note that the base assembles inside the sides and front, with the front set inside the sides.

Hold the front in place with two #6 x 1½-inch round-head-brass wood screws placed about 10 inches up from the bottom, one on each side. This placement allows the front to swing out for easy cleaning. The roof screws down to the sides.

Size variations (reducing the front height and side width to 6 inches each, with other reductions in proportion, for example) are possible for smaller birds, and the birdhouse is an easy one to make in small production runs. Just remember to fit the entry hole to the desired bird.

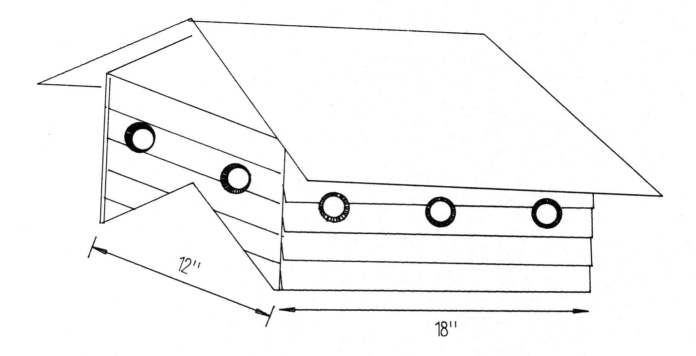

Illus. 71. Cupola. This simple cupola-style birdhouse is most useful for martins. Cut the design to match your existing roofline, and construct it using boards as clapboards or actual clapboards, if you want.

Shingle the roof in your choice of material, or use a metal roofing.

The interior is a simple drop in grid made to divide the cupola into the number of rooms you desire (the indicated size is suggested as near maximum for most houses).

You'll need roof framing only in cases of extreme overall size, or if you use very light (¼-inch thickness) roof sheathing. Framing is a good idea if you use metal roofing and the overall roof size exceeds 18 inches in any dimension.

Wall framing may be done, if needed (it is needed if overall cupola size passes 24 inches in any dimension). Use 2 x 2 material.

Columned Martin House

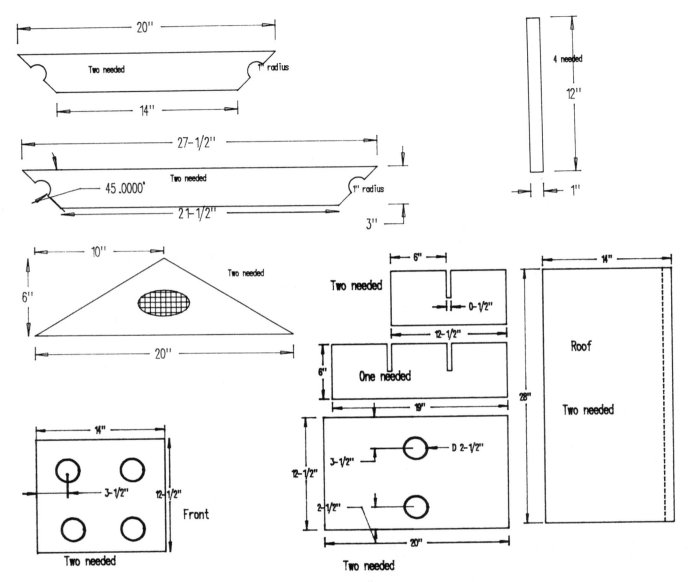

Illus. 72. Columned Martin House. The 27½-inch x 20-inch base is not shown. Cut two, one for use as a floor directly under the roof. Use ¾-inch Exterior plywood for the floors.

Cut the roof pieces as shown and bevel them to fit the gable ends, or cut them as two different-sized pieces and butt-joint.

If you butt-joint the pieces, cut one piece to the dimensions shown, and the second piece ¾-inch wider—14¾ inches instead of 14 inches.

Use hardware cloth or standard aluminum or fiberglass house-bug screening to cover the ellipse on the gable end. The ellipses provide ventilation, but they may be replaced by entry holes in each gable end and a central divider,

to provide fourteen units instead of a dozen. If you take the ellipses out, drill ¼-inch ventilation holes on both gable ends, 1 inch up and 2 inches in from bottom outside corners, and make the same-size holes in the divider used.

The columns shown are 1-inch hardwood dowels. Turning the dowels may give a more decorative effect.

Assemble with butt joints, except for the egg-crate dividers, which use slots. Sides fit inside the front and back, and may be nailed or screwed in place—screws allow easier take-down for cleaning.

Use ½-inch pine, cedar or redwood for the egg-crate dividers.

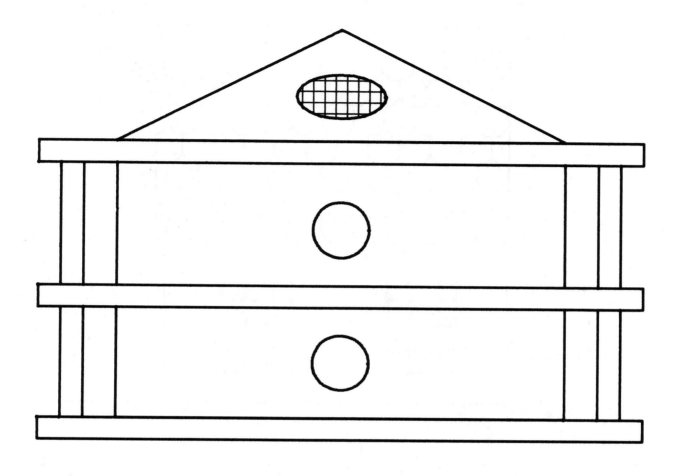

Illus. 73. Assembled Appearance. It is suggested that the house be painted white to resemble older plantation-style homes (Tara, anyone?). You may also wish to add a second, inner set of columns.

Shingled Birdhouse

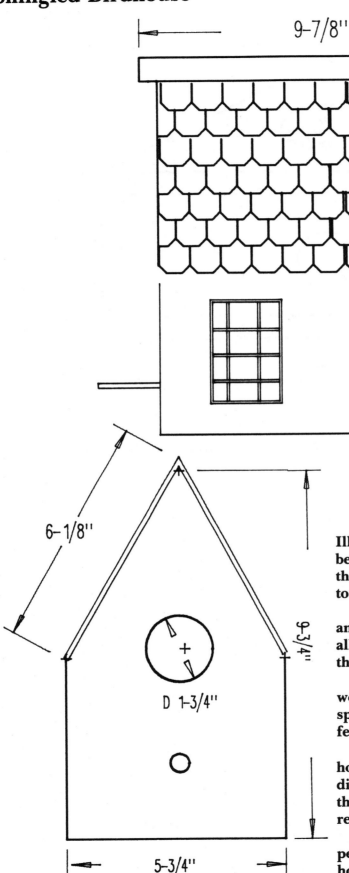

9-7/8"

0-5/8"

4-3/4"

6-1/8"

9-3/4"

D 1-3/4"

5-3/4"

Illus. 74. Shingled Birdhouse. The base may be an insert style, but an exterior mount makes the house simpler to set on a pole, and easier to clean out as well.

The front and the back are the same size, and the sides fit into them with butt joints. To allow some roof and gable overhang, make them 8⅞-inches long by 4¾-inches high.

This is a general birdhouse, using octagonal wooden shingles. It is suitable for many bird species, if the entry hole is drilled in the different sizes (see chart on page 124).

The shingles should soak no less than 24 hours in preservative (I used Zar Wood Conditioner), allowed to dry, and then attached to the roof with hot-melt glue or epoxy for best results.

If a brace block is placed inside the roof peak, this design may also be a hanging birdhouse.

Illus. 76. Mark shingle lines before gluing on shingles.

Illus. 75. Setting assembled roof in place. Note that whatever wood was available was what I used for this birdhouse. The body is plywood, while the roof is redwood.

Illus. 77. Overlap shingles as shown. I'm using thermoplastic glue here, and would recommend it as the easiest, fastest and most durable choice.

One-Storey Chalet

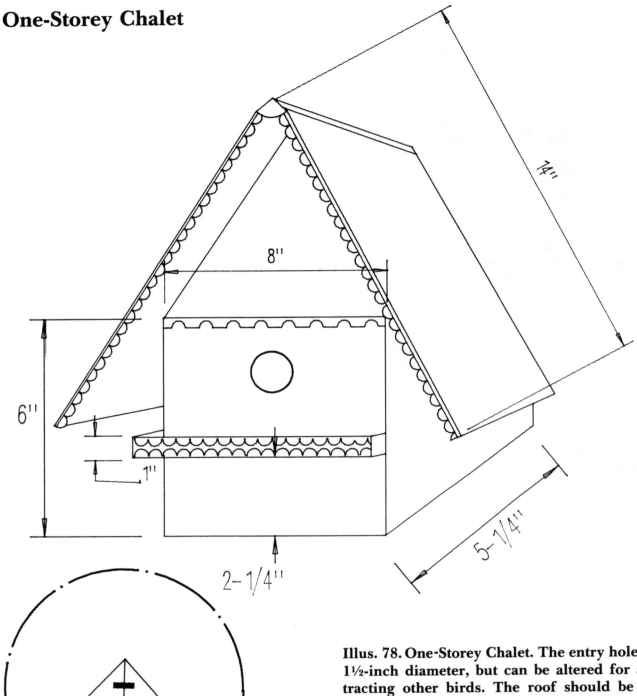

8"

14"

6"

1"

2-1/4"

5-1/4"

Roof is a splined mitre to add
strength for removals and replacements
after cleaning.

Illus. 78. One-Storey Chalet. The entry hole is 1½-inch diameter, but can be altered for attracting other birds. The roof should be at least 6½-inches deep. Make the roof with a splined mitre to add strength for removals and replacements, after cleaning. If you don't want to mess with splined mitre accuracy, simply add a brace block inside. The sides fit inside the front and the back.

Scrollwork may be painted on the balcony, but cut the trim or roof eaves with a scroll or saber saw. Repeat the pattern at the rear.

Make the roof as a unit to lift off, for easy cleaning. Use 1-inch (nominal) wood for the roof: shingles may be painted or glued on.

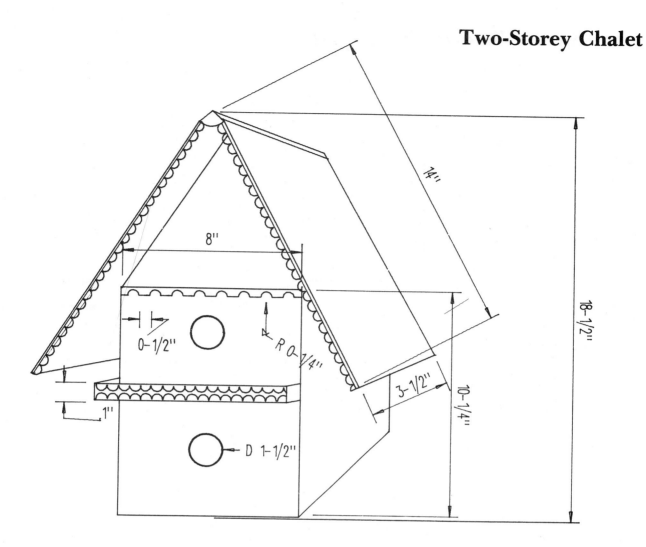

Two-Storey Chalet

Illus. 79. Two-Storey Chalet. In the model the entry holes are 1½-inch diameter, though you can alter it for birds you prefer to attract and house. The roof is a splined mitre to add strength for removals and replacements after cleaning.

To make the second storey floor removable, simply nail or glue in a cleat at each corner for the floor board to rest upon.

Scrollwork can be painted on the balcony, but the trim on the roof eaves needs to be cut with a scroll saw or saber saw. Repeat the pattern at the rear.

Make the roof as a unit, splined for lift-off strength to give easy inside cleaning. Hold it on the sides with two #6 x 1½-inch round-head screws.

Use 1-inch (nominal) wood for the roof. Shingles may be painted on or glued on (dollhouse shingles are good, and come in several patterns).

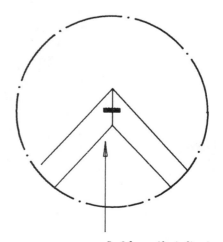

Roof is a splined mitre to add strength for removals and replacements after cleaning.

Gingerbread Victorian Birdhouse

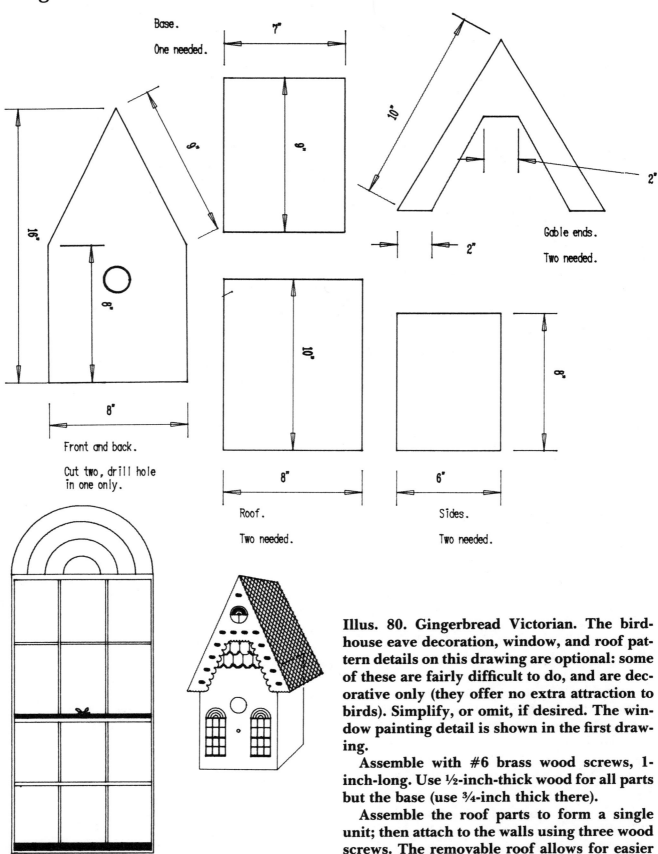

Base.
One needed.

7"

9"

9"

10"

2"

Gable ends.
Two needed.

2"

16"

9"

8"

Front and back.

Cut two, drill hole
in one only.

10"

8"

Roof.

Two needed.

8"

6"

Sides.

Two needed.

Window pattern detail

Illus. 80. Gingerbread Victorian. The birdhouse eave decoration, window, and roof pattern details on this drawing are optional: some of these are fairly difficult to do, and are decorative only (they offer no extra attraction to birds). Simplify, or omit, if desired. The window painting detail is shown in the first drawing.

Assemble with #6 brass wood screws, 1-inch-long. Use ½-inch-thick wood for all parts but the base (use ¾-inch thick there).

Assemble the roof parts to form a single unit; then attach to the walls using three wood screws. The removable roof allows for easier clean out.

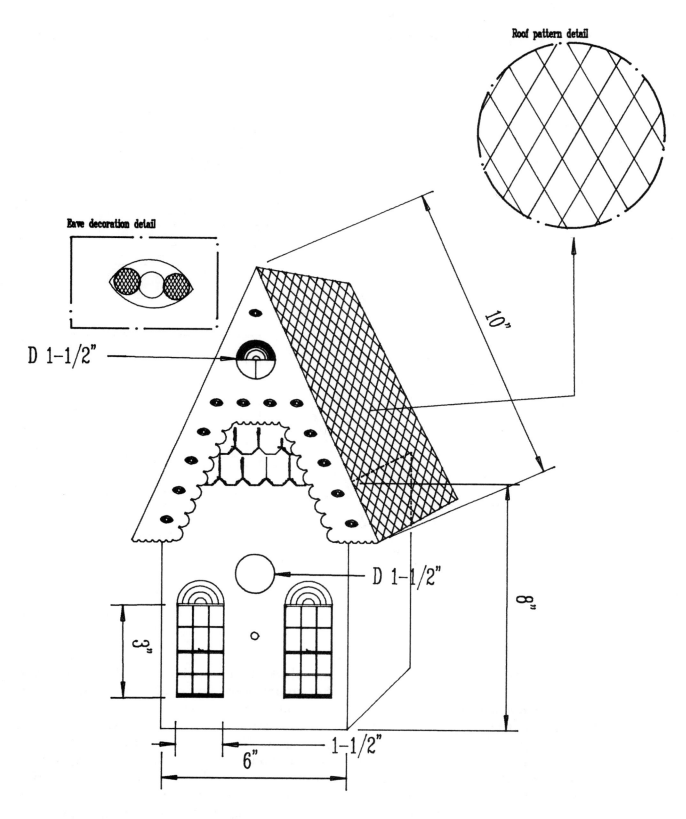

Roof pattern detail

Eave decoration detail

D 1-1/2"

10"

D 1-1/2"

8"

3"

6"

1-1/2"

Illus. 81. Shingles can go on with epoxy or heated adhesives and are standard dollhouse octagonal or fish scale styles. The varied designs, as noted on the first drawing, are painted on. Radii for the eave cutouts are in the first drawing.

Gambrel Roof Nuthatch House

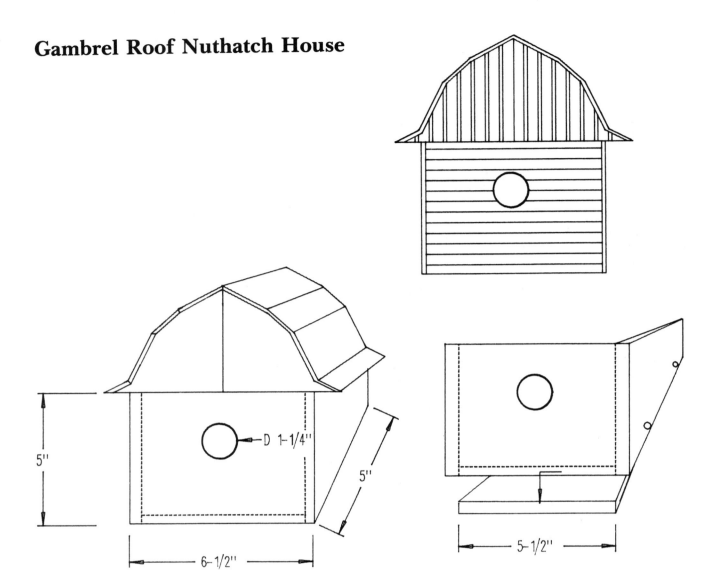

Illus. 82. Gambrel Roof Nuthatch House. The house depth and length are readily and simply variable, making the house suitable for a number of birds. For example, use a 2-inch entry hole, and a 6-inch square base with a 10-inch depth, and this house is suitable for crested flycatchers. For a wood duck, cut the entry hole a 3-inch ellipse (about 2 inches high), increase the overall size to about a foot square at the base (externally), using ¾-inch lumber, and provide a 2-foot-high overall height—assembling the roof open on the base (roof assembly detail is on the next page).

The barn siding may be done any of several ways. The easiest is to use redwood stain; then use black stain or paint to apply vertical and horizontal lines. You could also stain or paint dollhouse siding; then trim it to the appropriate size, after which apply it with a thermal glue gun. This technique is more fun. Of course, you might also cut the siding to size from ⅜- or ¼-inch solid wood stock, miniaturizing standard board siding, after which apply it with epoxy or a hot-glue gun, piece by piece. Attach the bottom (5½- x 4-inches) with four screws (brass or galvanized). The two front screws allow the floor to pivot down for a quick clean out. Use #6 x 1-inch, or similar-sized, screw.

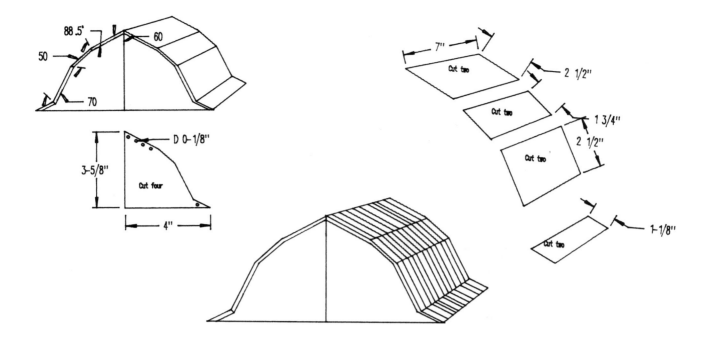

Illus. 83. Gambrel Roof Detail. Generally, barn roofs are made of sheets of aluminum or galvanized steel today. If you wish to go the lengths of fabricating an authentic tin roof, I would suggest locating old printing plates. Local printing plants and small newspapers often have these photo-offset plates in good supply. They are cheap, easily shaped, and more than reasonably durable.

I strongly suggest using some form of ½-inch-thick (or more) insulating material under a metal roof. Summer cooling needs help with tin roofing. If you use insulation, move the ventilation holes down ½ inch or so.

Metal roofing also requires purlins (simple struts) along the edges of the roof, but will cut out the need for accurate bevel rips on wood-roofing materials. Overlap the metal top over bottom, about ¼ to ½ inch, and seal with a silicone or mastic cement.

Metal trims more easily with a good, sharp utility knife and straightedge on a hard surface than with tin snips. Mark the line to be cut—scoring moderately hard—three times; then bend gently until it parts. The edge is far less ragged that way.

Vertical roof changes should be made proportionately for an accurate fit. The best method is to make a cardboard template of one half of an end and experiment with section lengths until you reach the right size. Measure and maintain dimensions (including all angles), and you'll have an accurately laid-out roof.

Any durable wood ¼-inch or thicker will do. Accuracy of cuts is less essential with thinner woods which may, in fact, be overlapped (top over bottom, which means applying the bottom first) and left with standard edges. Change the cut angles so that each cut is half the included angle.

Assemble with brass brads, epoxy, resorcinol adhesives, or a thermal glue gun. Resorcinol needs clamping, which is difficult with this shape, so the hot-glue or the epoxy methods are preferable.

Length dimensions can be changed as you wish. To keep the same roof style simply maintain all angles and cut things longer.

Start assembly with the base board; then attach the post mounting board. Drill ⅛-inch or ¼-inch holes as shown, if a solid base is used.

Older barns may have shake or shingle roofs, so you may wish to modify the design to that pattern. If not, use an aluminum-based paint—darker paints are best. A number of the wilder species are badly frightened by bright colors.

Log Cabin

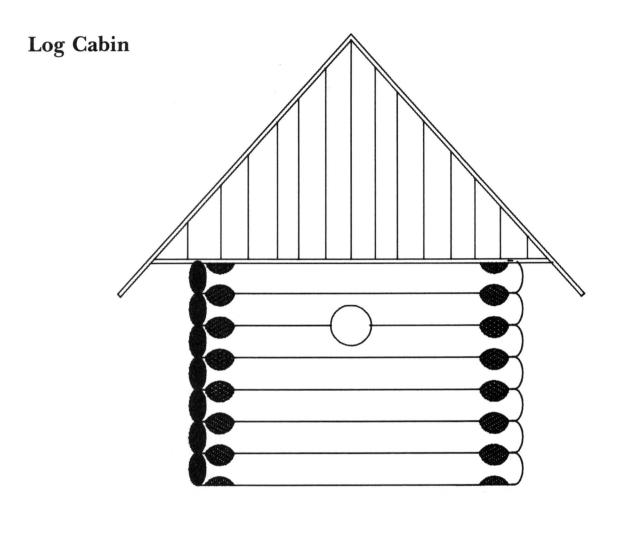

Detail of cut dowel.

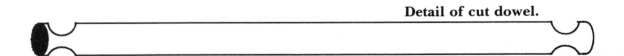

Illus. 84. Log Cabin. Made from notched dowels, this cabin presents fewer unchinked spots to the wind than would one using small branches. Use 1-inch dowels for the walls, to the appropriate lengths (add 1½ inches to that for notch and overhang at each end).

Soak the siding and the dowels at least 24 hours in preservative or coat with stain such as Zar Rain Stain.

Fasten the dowels together with brass brads through the notches into dowel below.

The roof is ¼-inch or ⅜-inch plywood, and may be covered with dollhouse shingles or "shakes" (trimmed to scale cedar shim stock). Attach with epoxy or hot-melt glue.

The floor is ¾-inch plywood, cut to fit the outside. Drill the center hole after assembly. If it doesn't fall exactly on top of the arc of a dowel, use rubber cement to hold a flat piece of wood directly above the drilling area, and drill through the flat piece and into the dowels.

The house may be made with ¾-inch dowels, or even ½-inch, to suit smaller birds.

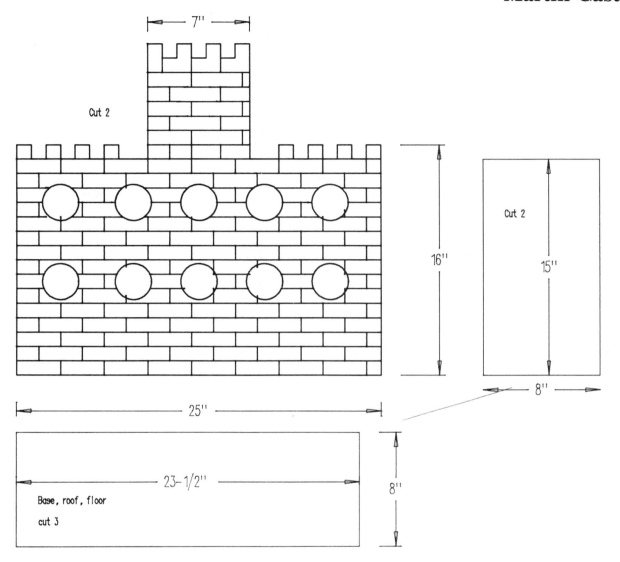

Illus. 85. Martin Castle. The 10-unit martin castle can be increased in size quite easily. Simply make the base, the roof, and the sides twice their present 8-inch dimensions, drill the back as a second front, and place a divider of ½-inch lumber between the two units, in addition to the floor and present dividers.

I would suggest, even for the simple plan presented, using egg-crate style dividers, cutting and fitting after the base, front and back are assembled. Dimensional quirks thus are no problem. Use ½-inch material for the dividers, and ¾-inch for the floor and all other parts.

The roof needs to be pressure-treated and tightly sealed. For this reason, make the bottom removable, using #6 x 1½-inch wood screws—four, round-head—for easy clean out. Drill a couple of ventilation holes for each nest unit, and make sure the base can drain. Drill at least two ¼-inch-diameter holes in each nesting cavity floor section, and this is taken care of.

Painting the stone-masonry look is simple. Use a flat grey background–flat paints and stains are always better with birdhouses and feeders, as some birds are badly scared by glossy, bright paints–and draw the black lines with a felt-tipped marker, or thin paint brush (I used felt-tip pens because my skills with art brushes are non-existent).

Owl Hoot Saloon

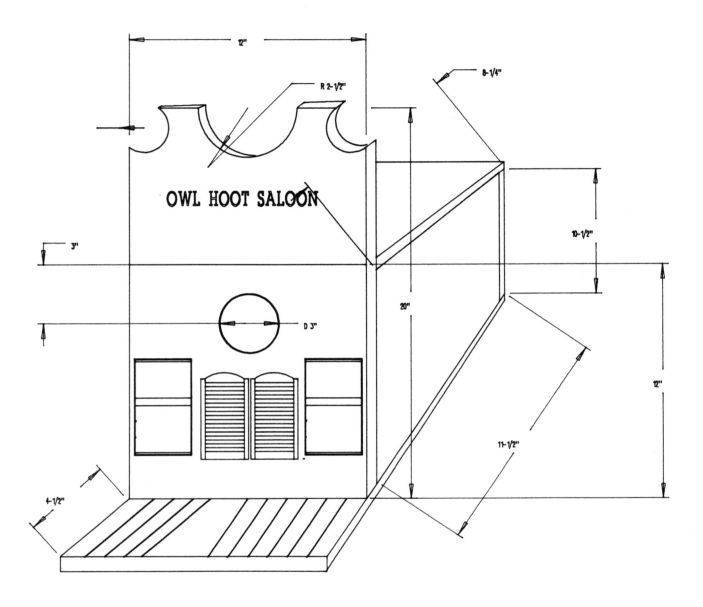

OWL HOOT SALOON

Illus. 86. Owl Hoot Saloon. This replica of the Hollywood version of an Old West saloon makes a fine, whimsical birdhouse for large birds. The patterns are more difficult to draw for smaller versions, but it can be adapted.

The painted windows may be replaced with, or added to, painted bat-wing doors.

Butt joints and nails are used everywhere, except for three #6 x 1½-inch-brass wood

screws to hold the roof on, which allows an easy clean out when needed.

Easily variable size for different species of birds, plus easy assembly, along with the unique—as far as I know, anyway—design might make this birdhouse suitable for short production runs. The pattern and lettering dimensions could be changed and produced from templates.

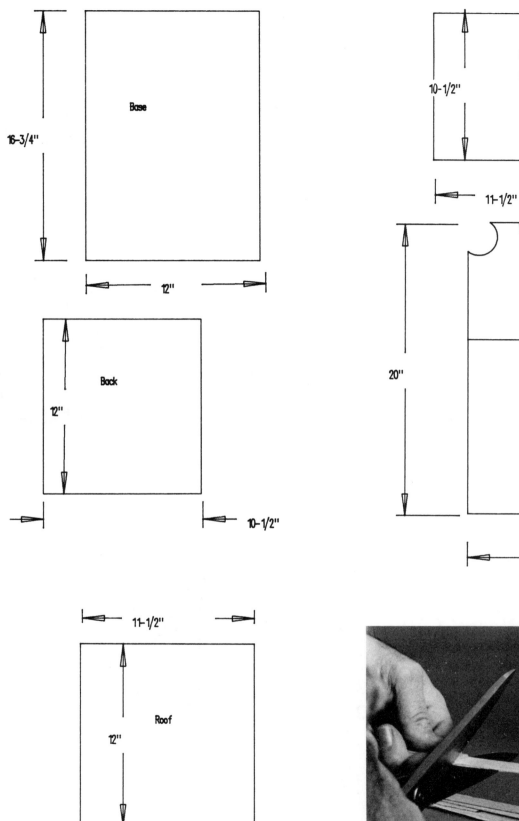

Base

16-3/4"

12"

Back

12"

10-1/2"

Side

Cut two

10-1/2"

11-1/2"

20"

Front

12"

11-1/2"

Roof

12"

Illus. 87. Cutting boards for the walk. These are dollhouse siding sections.

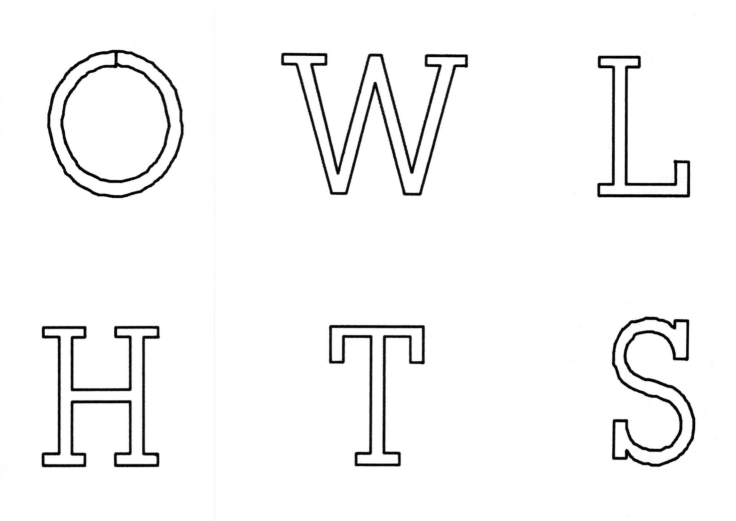

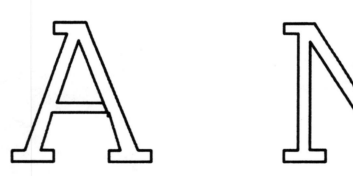

Illus. 88. Lettering for the saloon (actual size).

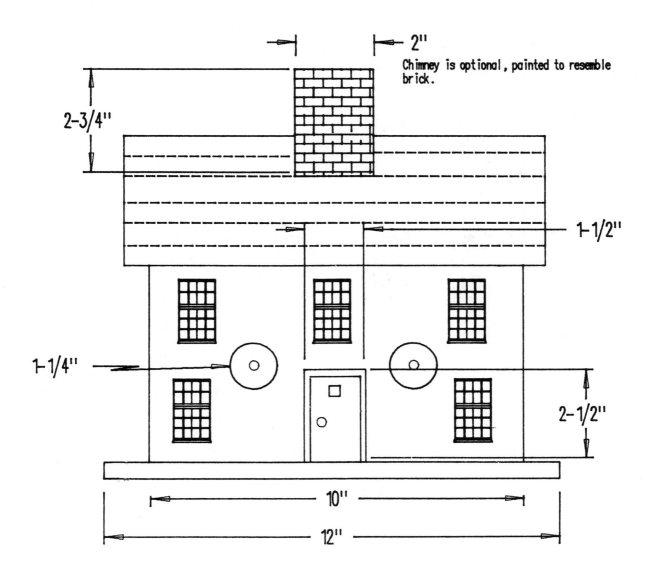

2"

Chimney is optional, painted to resemble brick.

2-3/4"

1-1/2"

1-1/4"

2-1/2"

10"

12"

Illus. 89. New England Salt Box. As designed, this birdhouse is suitable for any species that will accept a second nest in the same box (with divider insert, of course). Reduce the dimensions by one-third and use a single hole (centered) and the Salt Box design is suitable for many more species. The roof may use painted shingles or dollhouse shingles.

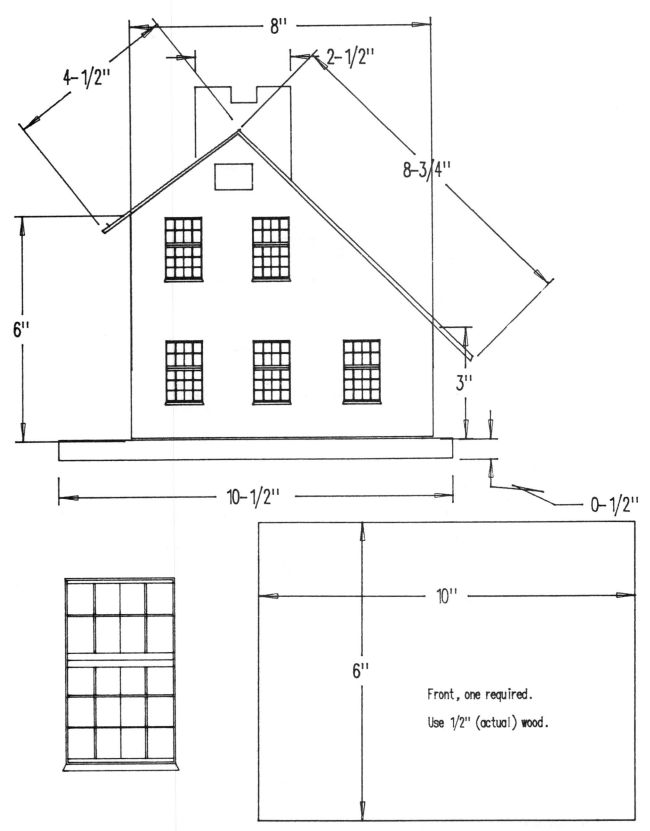

Illus. 90. The optional window pattern is 1¾-inches high by 1-inch wide, with a traditional six over nine panes. You could also simply paint in blank windows, or leave the front and sides blank.

The chimney is optional, and painted to resemble brick.

Entry holes shown are 1¼ inches in diameter. See chart for other applicable sizes.

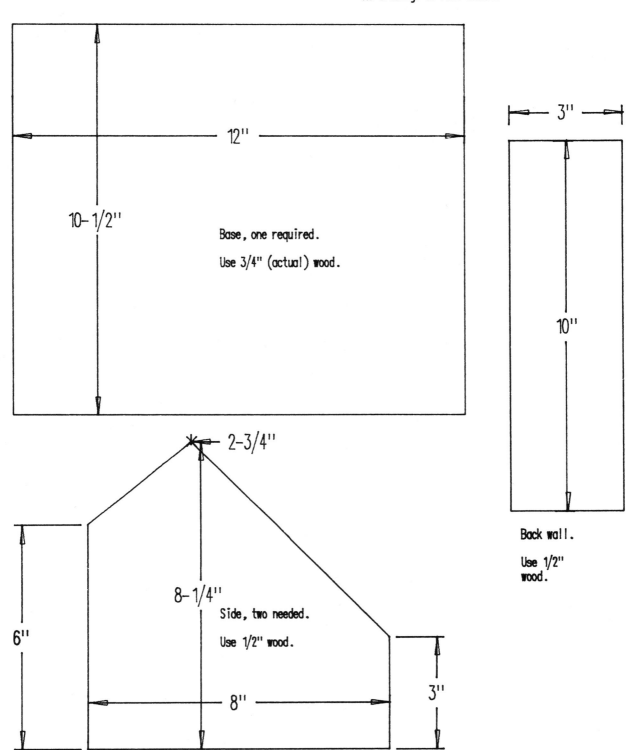

Front roof: 3/4" material, 4-1/2" x 11-1/2"
Back roof: 3/4" x 8-3/4" x 11-1/2"   No drawings of roof shown.

12"

10-1/2"

Base, one required.

Use 3/4" (actual) wood.

3"

10"

Back wall.

Use 1/2" wood.

2-3/4"

8-1/4"

Side, two needed.

Use 1/2" wood.

6"

8"

3"

Illus. 91. Salt Box. Part patterns. One base is needed, of ¾-inch thick stock. One front is required, of ½-inch stock. The back wall is also ½-inch stock, as are the two identical sides.

7
Bird-Feeder Designs

Simple Ground Feeder

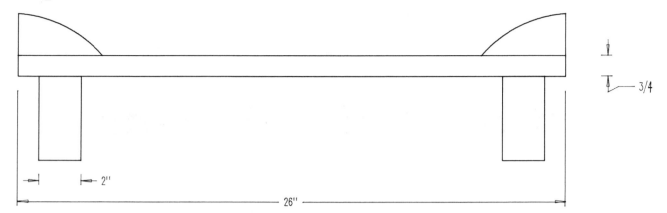

Illus. 92. Simple Ground Feeder. This is ¾-inch Exterior plywood, and uses a large square or rectangle, with blocks placed at each corner to keep the bottom off the lawn. The blocks may be 2 inches square, and up to 4 inches high. The rectangle (or square) itself should be no less than 18 inches in its smallest dimension. The corner arcs are ½-inch plywood or solid wood, and cut down wind scattering of seed. They can be made as large or as small as you wish.

Flying Wing Ground Feeder

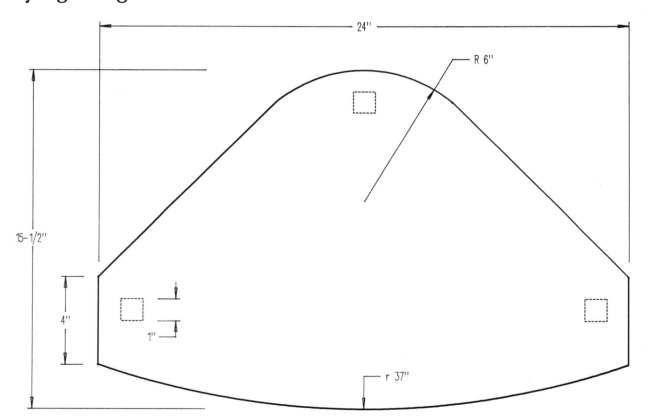

Illus. 93. Flying Wing Ground Feeder. This is almost identical to the simple ground feeder, except for its shape. Use a 37-inch radius for the bottom curve, and a 6-inch radius at top.

The entire feeder can be made from ¾-inch Exterior plywood, and can be raised off the ground as far as desired.

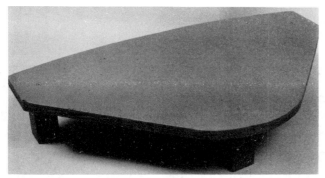

Illus. 93 A. Flying wing feeder.

Quick Covered Feeder

Illus. 94. Quick Covered Feeder. This quickly made feeder uses plywood, or any other wood you have on hand, in appropriate sizes. The only parts not shown are the roof supports, which need to be of at least 1- x ¾-inch lumber.

The base is ¾-inch Exterior plywood. The roof may be ½-inch or heavier (heavier is better to hold down warping) plywood. Assembly with screws is best, though nails and glue may be used.

The feeder is designed primarily for pole mounting, but needs only a ridge brace for hanging. Stain or paint in fairly dark colors.

Illus. 94 A. Quick covered feeder.

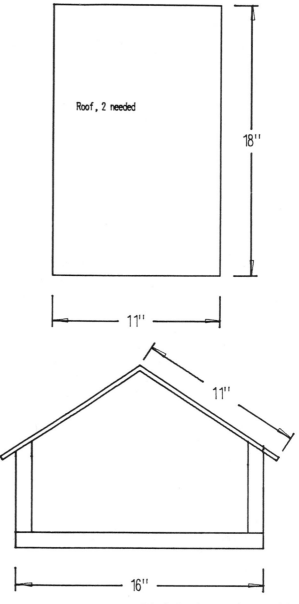

Roof, 2 needed

18"

11"

11"

16"

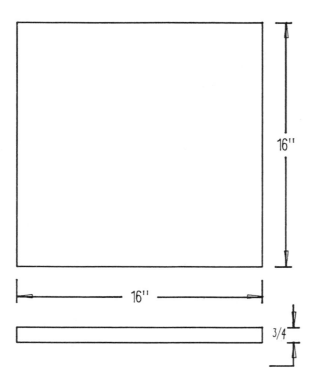

16"

16"

3/4

Suet Feeder

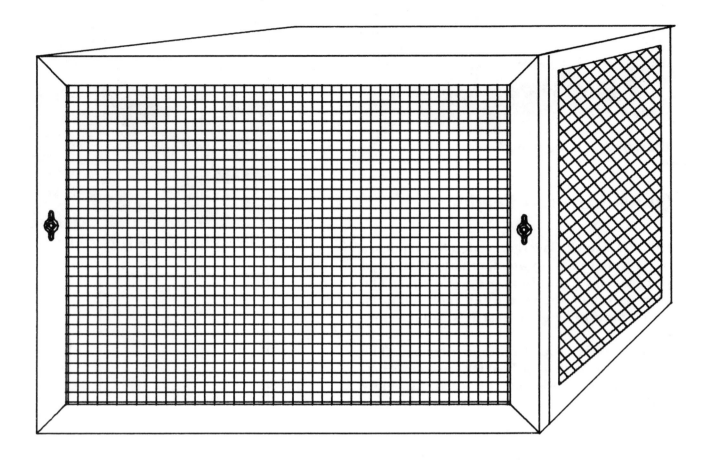

Illus. 95. Suet Feeder. This remains relatively simple, while using nicely mitred joints to hold the "door" together. The backs of all the wood parts are rabbeted to hold a hardware cloth with a ⅛-inch or ¼-inch mesh.

Make the rabbet about ¼- x ¼-inch, depending on your router bit availability (the cut may also be made on a table saw with a dado head; with multiple passes of a single blade; or with a saw cut and a chisel). The top of the suet feeder is solid ¼-inch or ¾-inch Exterior plywood, as is the bottom. Both are rabbeted into their respective frames, and both give racking strength to the unit.

If you make the feeder about 8-inches square, you can make four sides for hardware mesh nearly identical, except that the front door side mounts onto two machine screws set in the mating sides. Use thumbscrews (#6) to attach the door.

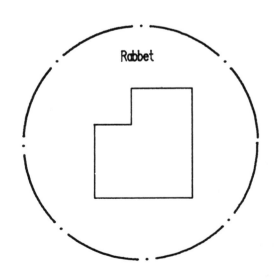

Rabbet

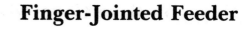

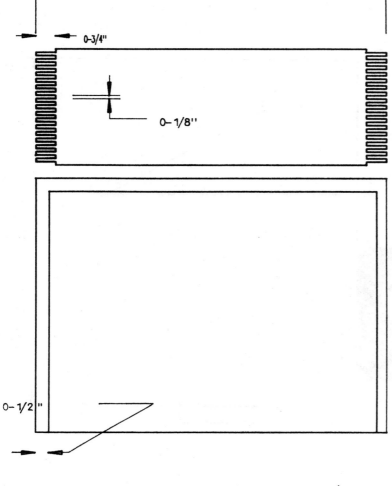

13"

0-3/4"

0-1/8"

0-1/2"

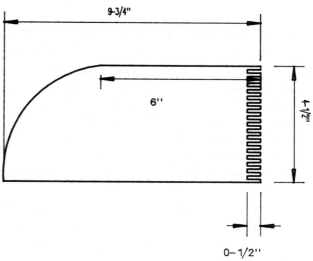

9-3/4"

6"

4-1/2"

0-1/2"

Illus. 96. Finger-Jointed Feeder. This simple feeder design is more interesting because of the finger joints on the back and sides. Once assembled, the back and sides are set into the ½-inch rabbet cut around three edges of the base, using glue and nails. The design looks best in cedar, but partial sapwood redwood also looks good.

Hexagon-Base Covered Feeder

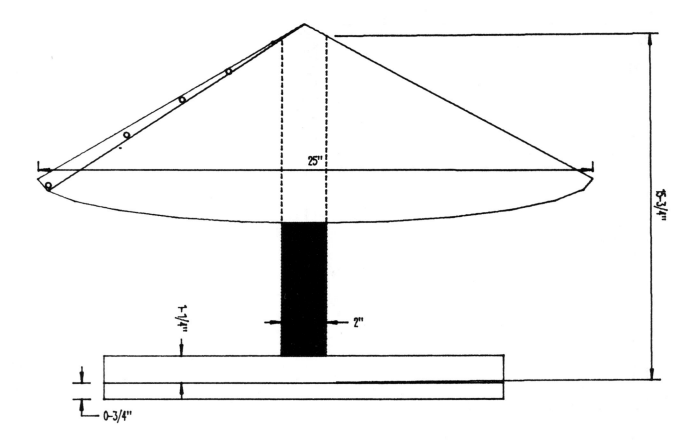

Illus. 97. Hexagon-Base Covered Feeder. The base sides are 10 inches each. Use Exterior or Marine plywood. Do NOT use pressure-treated wood for the base or any parts of it.

You can hang or post-mount this feeder. If you post-mount, use 2-inch PVC pipe and a second pipe flange to attach the feeder to the post, or you can attach the base to the post; then screw in center post flange and put on the roof.

Attach the roof to the pipe with Pop-riveted metal tabs screwed to the post. Screw the tabs to the post first; then drill and rivet the top seam.

The roof is sheet aluminum, fastened with Pop rivets.

Note 120° angle. Cut the angles to 60° to get a 120° included angle.

Cut the sides from ¾-inch cedar or redwood, after it is ripped to 1¼-inch height.

Attach the sides with epoxy, nails, hot glue, or screws as you wish.

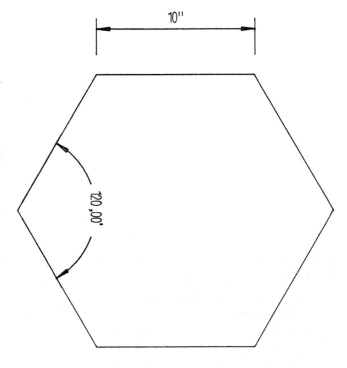

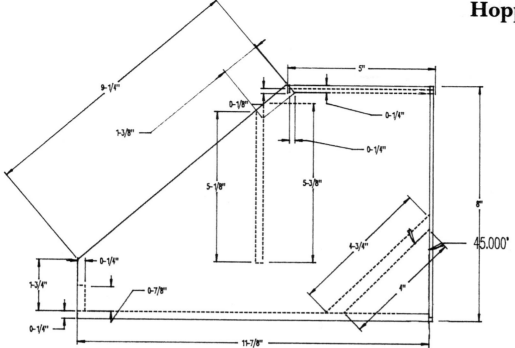

Illus. 98. Hopper Feeder. Using ½-inch and ¼-inch stock, this feeder is lightweight, but offers good capacity that can be readily varied by making the feeder wider or narrower. The back is ⅛-inch plywood or hardboard, and sits in a ⅛-inch rabbet. Use a ³⁄₃₂ non-brass nail or pin for roof pivot pins, in 1-inch lengths.

Large Hopper Feeder

Illus. 99. Large Hopper Feeder. This is quite easy to construct, and uses ¾-inch (true) lumber or plywood.

The hinge at the top of the feeder may be replaced with a rubber strip and tacked in place, though both the appearance and the durability will drop. The width is up to you, though I would recommend no less than 10 inches, and probably no more than 18. The windbreaks on the sides are optional, depending on where you place the feeder, and the wind in your area. They may be stained contrasting colors (if color is used) to add visual interest.

This feeder may be pole mounted, side mounted on a building, or modified for use as a hanging feeder. Add one-half-inch eyes on each side, about 8 to 9 inches up and as close to the point of balance as possible, or use two eyes to each side and forget about the point of balance, if you wish.

The hopper front may be Plexiglas, so you can easily determine feed levels, or wood.

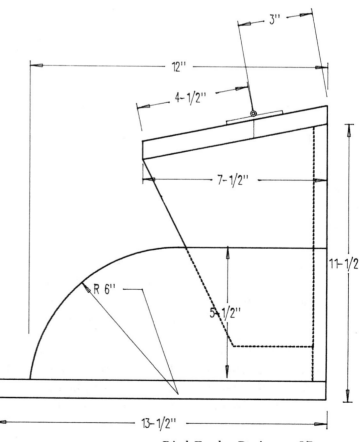

Thistle Feeder

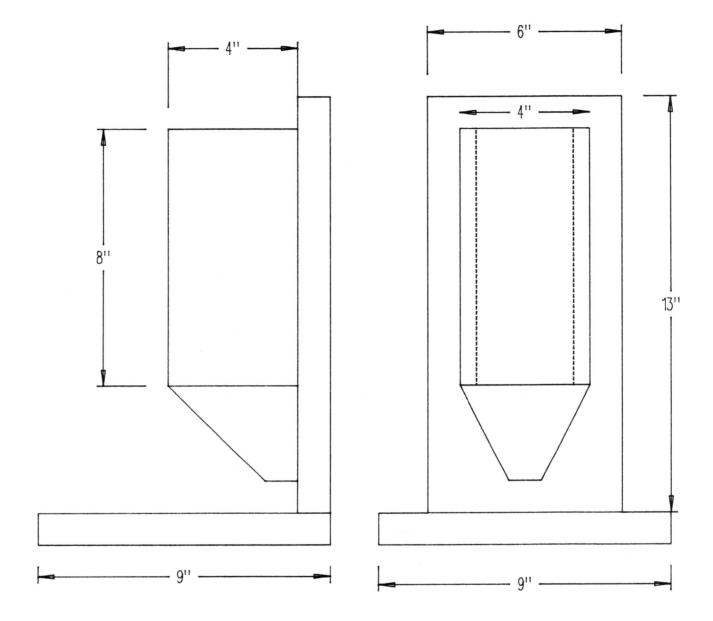

Illus. 100. Thistle Feeder. The lower portion of this feeder, as shown in the drawing, is meant to be made of plastic, but I tried three different versions of acrylic, and all turned out to be expensive garbage, shattering no matter what method was used to cut them. Thus, my thistle feeder is made of cedar and redwood (base and back) with no plastic used.

Attach the optional roof with a Stanley 2½-inch x ¾-inch solid brass hinge.

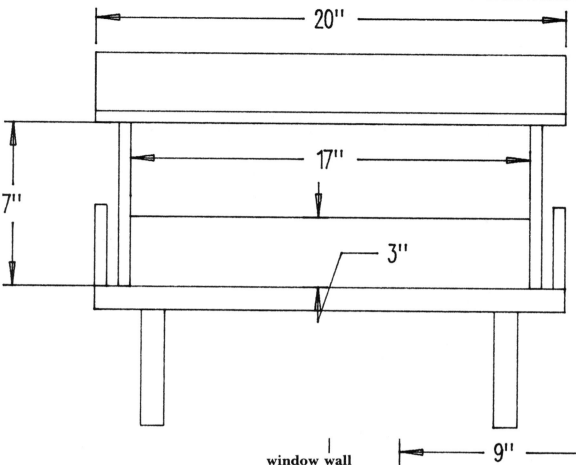

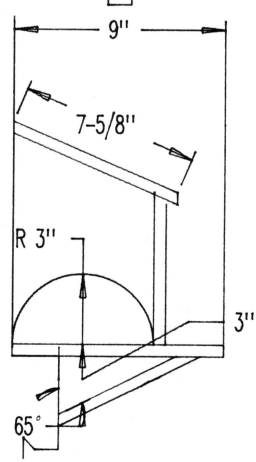

**Illus. 101. Windowsill Feeder. This feeder is
designed to be braced against a window with
two braces. These should be cut to size—obvi-
ously the variables in the size and material of
windowsills require different lengths and fas-
teners.**

Use ¾-inch stock. The arcs, or half-circles,
mount with butt joints on the baseboard, and
serve as protection from gusty winds, helping
to keep the feed in place. Use a 3-inch radius
for the arcs. The baseboard should be 20 x 9
inches and the backboard is 17 x 7 inches. The
backboard is essential to keep debris off the
window glass, and it fits against the back of the
half-circle sides, with butt joints.

Single- and double-hung windows need be
raised only 6 or 8 inches to refill feeder.

Pentagon Feeder

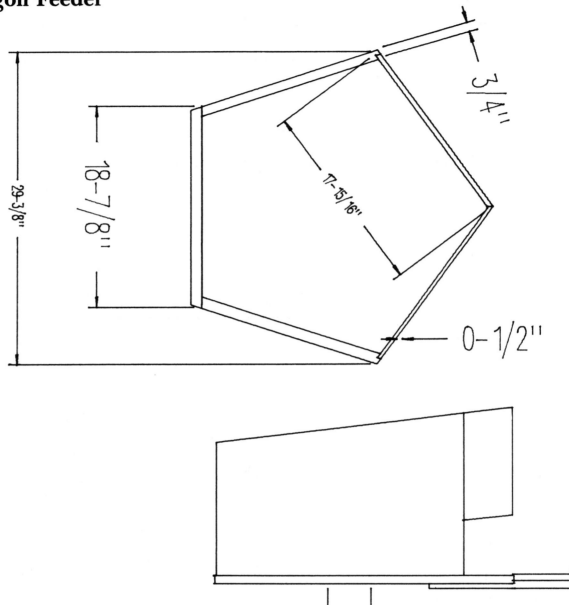

Illus. 102. Pentagon Feeder. This pentagon has nothing to do with war or weapons. The Plexiglas front is cut off well above the feed (2-inches minimum) to allow easy access. The top lifts off, and is secured with two thumb-screws or machine screws. It can be plywood or sheet aluminum.

The base, for pole mounting, offers a porch, extending the feeding area, with a small piece of half-round capping the edge.

The front sides are Plexiglas, cemented with model cement at the center to form a single pane. Use brass brads or screws to hold the plastic in the side rabbets.

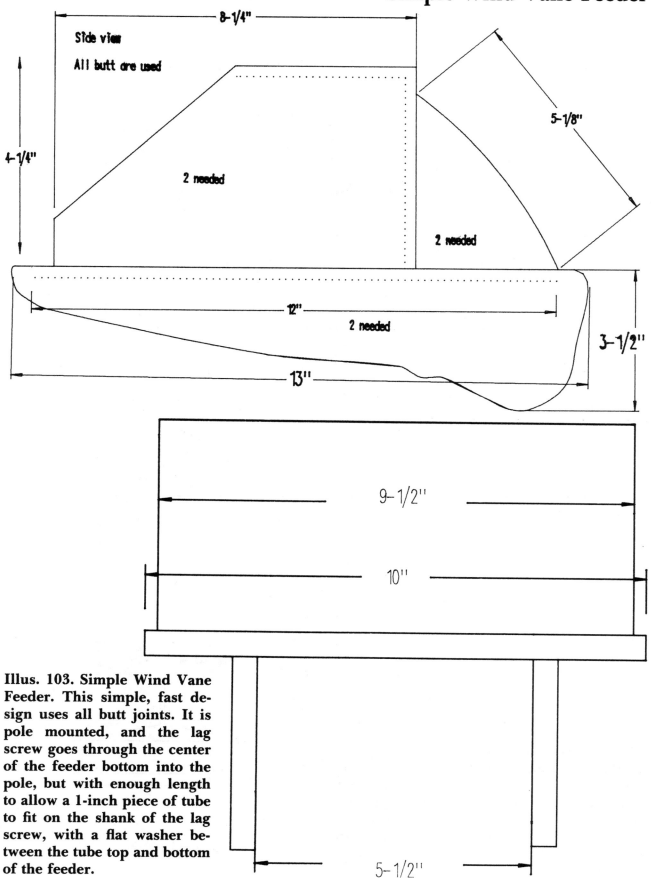

Illus. 103. Simple Wind Vane Feeder. This simple, fast design uses all butt joints. It is pole mounted, and the lag screw goes through the center of the feeder bottom into the pole, but with enough length to allow a 1-inch piece of tube to fit on the shank of the lag screw, with a flat washer between the tube top and bottom of the feeder.

Wind Vane Feeder

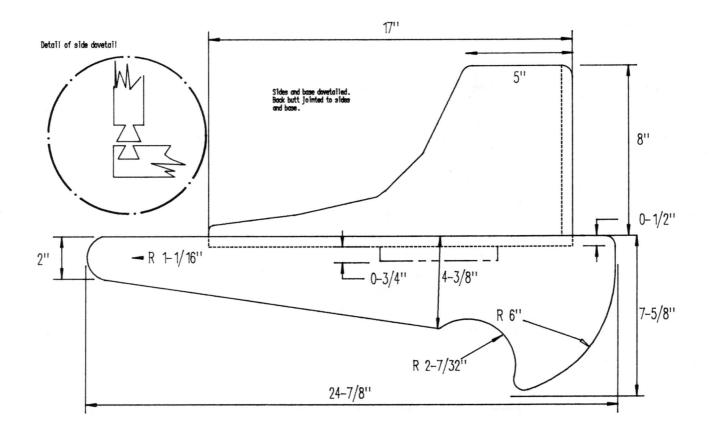

Detail of side dovetail

Sides and base dovetailed.
Back butt jointed to sides
and base.

17"

5"

8"

0-1/2"

2"

R 1-1/16"

0-3/4"

4-3/8"

R 6"

7-5/8"

R 2-7/32"

24-7/8"

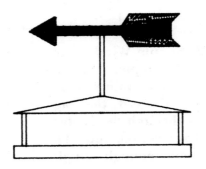

Illus. 104. Wind Vane Feeder. Similar in overall shape and mounting to the simpler wind vane feeder, this version uses dovetail joints to fix the sides and the back in place. These are easily cut on the router. This is a capacious feeder even in a width of only 1 foot. If you want more birds to feed, widen it to 2 feet, or even 30 inches.

Weather Vane Feeder

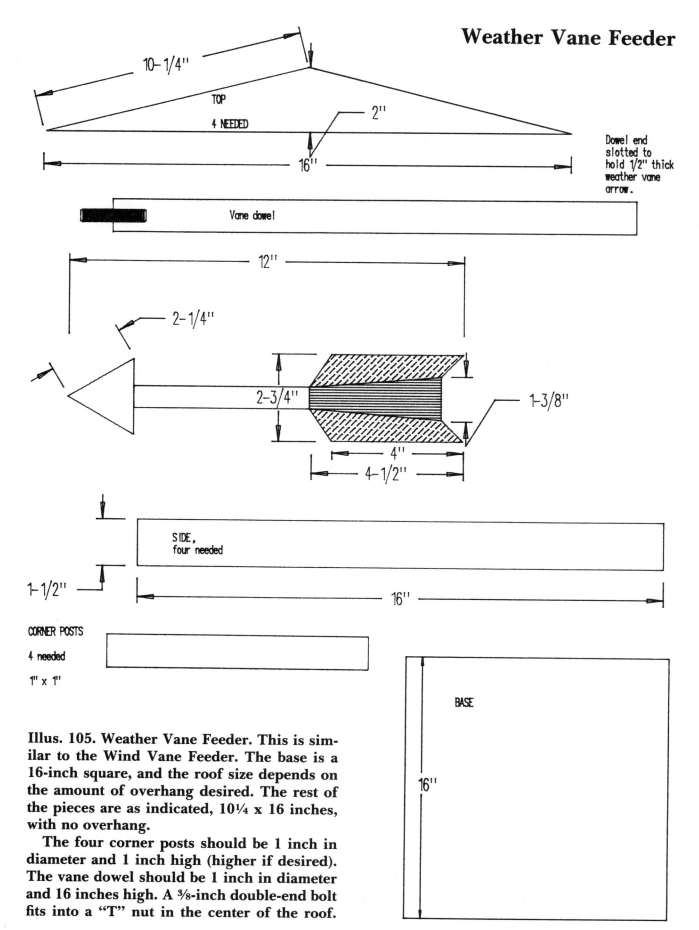

10-1/4"

TOP
4 NEEDED

2"

16"

Dowel end slotted to hold 1/2" thick weather vane arrow.

Vane dowel

12"

2-1/4"

2-3/4"

1-3/8"

4"

4-1/2"

SIDE,
four needed

1-1/2"

16"

CORNER POSTS

4 needed

1" x 1"

BASE

16"

Illus. 105. Weather Vane Feeder. This is similar to the Wind Vane Feeder. The base is a 16-inch square, and the roof size depends on the amount of overhang desired. The rest of the pieces are as indicated, 10¼ x 16 inches, with no overhang.

The four corner posts should be 1 inch in diameter and 1 inch high (higher if desired). The vane dowel should be 1 inch in diameter and 16 inches high. A ⅜-inch double-end bolt fits into a "T" nut in the center of the roof.

Four-Way Feeder

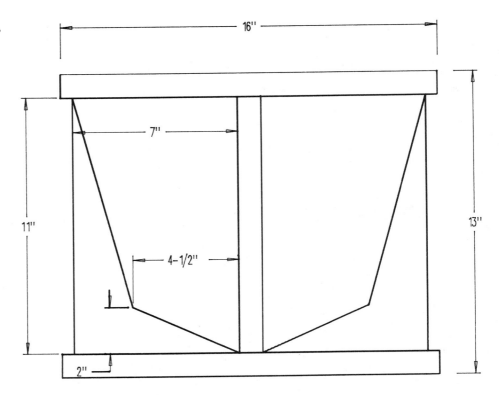

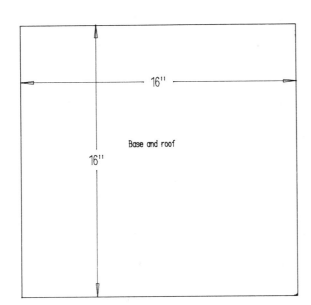

Base and roof

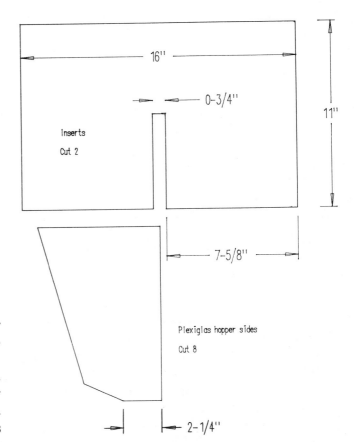

Inserts
Cut 2

Plexiglas hopper sides
Cut 8

Illus. 106. Four-Way Feeder. This clever feeder design allows four birds to feed at once without any crowding.

The base is a 16-inch square, as is the roof. The floor is a simple lift-off design, and may be screwed down between fillings, if you wish.

You'll need two inserts, each 16 x 11 inches with a ¾-inch-wide slit down the center. The best way to do these is to pad-cut them. You'll also need eight Plexiglas hopper sides, assembled as shown.

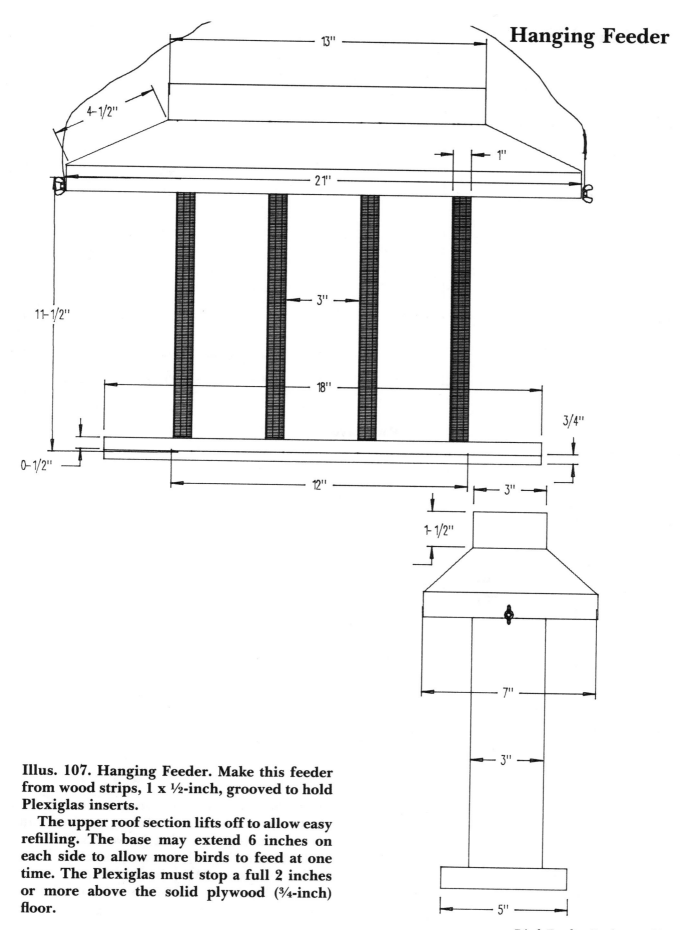

Hanging Feeder

Illus. 107. Hanging Feeder. Make this feeder from wood strips, 1 x ½-inch, grooved to hold Plexiglas inserts.

The upper roof section lifts off to allow easy refilling. The base may extend 6 inches on each side to allow more birds to feed at one time. The Plexiglas must stop a full 2 inches or more above the solid plywood (¾-inch) floor.

Shed Feeder

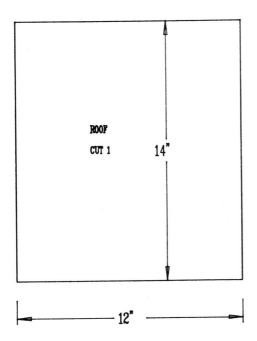

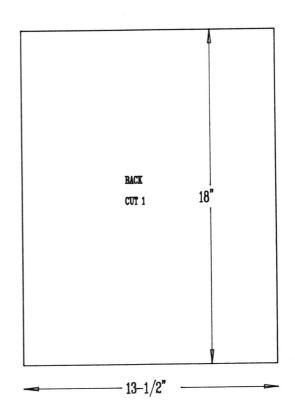

Parts layout

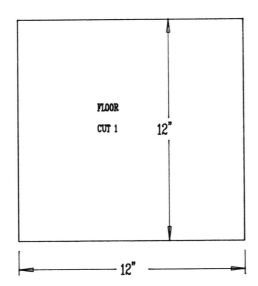

Illus. 108. Shed Feeder. Assemble the sides to the backboard first. Next, insert the floor and secure it, using 1½-inch x #6 wood screws, or nails. Finally, install the roof, attaching it in the same manner. All joints are butts.

Cut the sides from ¾-inch stock to dimensions shown on side view drawing.

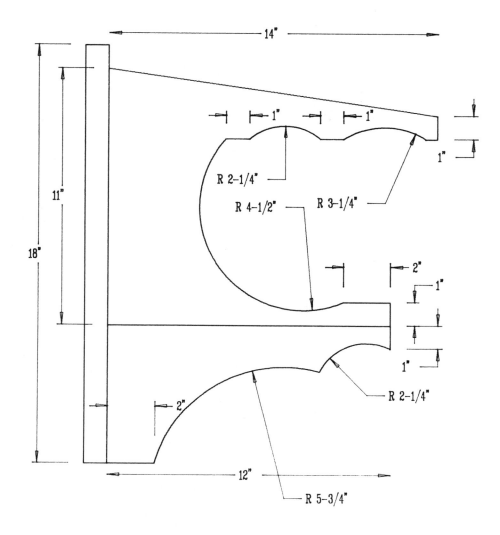

Illus. 109. Shed Feeder. Side View. Radii shown may be varied as you wish, and simple arcs may be substituted, as may almost any other pattern that still allows reasonable access to the seed.

Overall stock size required is 14- x 17-inches; and construction is far simpler if both side patterns are pad cut—that is, tape or tack the side pieces together, and make one cut for the pattern.

Pagoda

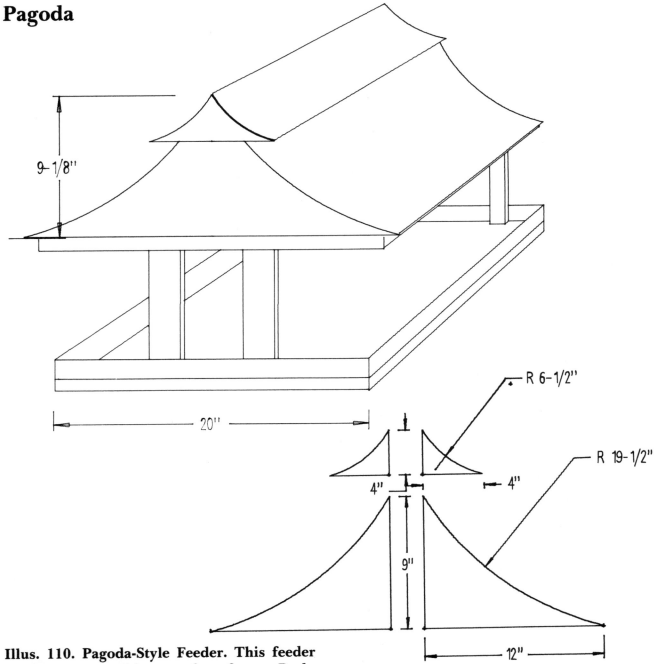

Illus. 110. Pagoda-Style Feeder. This feeder can be constructed in a number of ways. Probably the quickest is to make the length minimal, about 18 inches, and use the sheet aluminum as indicated, with attachment tabs, totally for the roof. The roof is also variable in length, but once it gets past 18 inches, you'll find a modification makes things stronger: use ¾-inch plywood rafters, cut the gable-end-piece shapes; then roll the sheet aluminum into those, attaching with either aluminum nails or sheet metal screws to hold in place. Use the roof frame as a securing point whether for the rafters or the tabs (use 1- x 2-inch tabs if the roof is all metal).

Mitre the corner pieces on the spill guard.

The base is ¾-inch Exterior plywood. Otherwise use 1¼-inch lumber. Adjust the lengths to fit coil stock—aluminum is easiest to work with; usually, it is found in 12-, 18-, 20- and 24-inch widths. Cut coil stock with a utility knife. Place a straightedge on the stock, with the material on a hard, smooth, surface. Move the knife along the edge at least three times, and bend it until it parts. To make bends that are sharp, use a straightedge, and run the utility knife firmly, but not hard, once across, then bend.

8
Bird Aids

Squirrel and Predator Guard

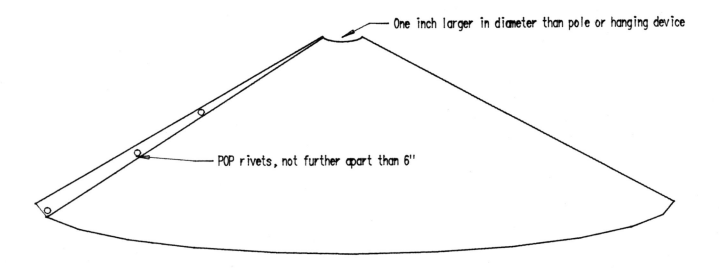

One inch larger in diameter than pole or hanging device

POP rivets, not further apart than 6"

Illus. 111. Squirrel and Predator Guard. For pole feeders, mount this below the feeder; for hanging feeders, mount it above. It should be made of 20 (or lighter) gauge sheet aluminum.

This should be at least six times the diameter of the pole around which it is mounted. If you mount it above the feeder, it need only be about 2 inches more in diameter than the largest feeder dimension.

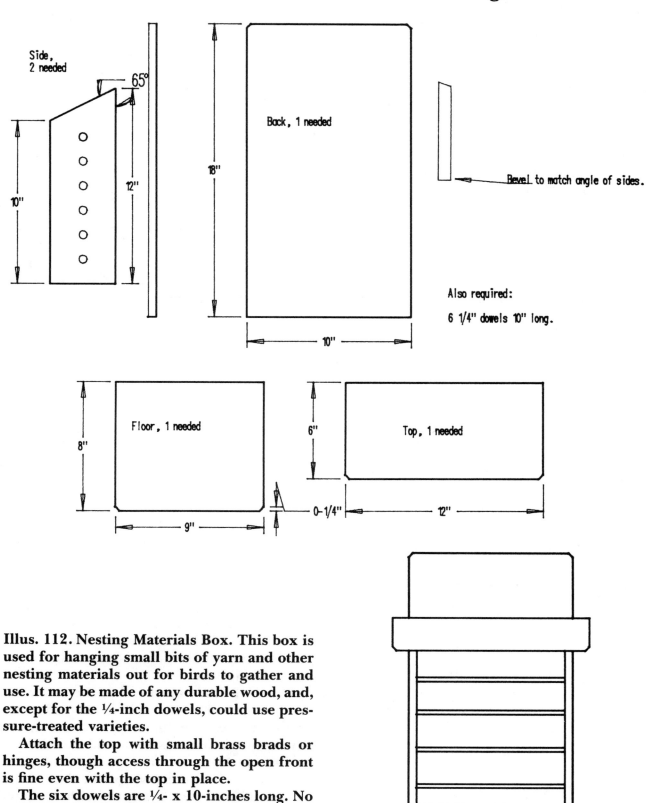

Side,
2 needed

65°

10"

12"

Back, 1 needed

18"

10"

Bevel to match angle of sides.

Also required:

6 1/4" dowels 10" long.

Floor, 1 needed

8"

9"

0-1/4"

Top, 1 needed

6"

12"

Illus. 112. Nesting Materials Box. This box is used for hanging small bits of yarn and other nesting materials out for birds to gather and use. It may be made of any durable wood, and, except for the ¼-inch dowels, could use pressure-treated varieties.

Attach the top with small brass brads or hinges, though access through the open front is fine even with the top in place.

The six dowels are ¼- x 10-inches long. No dimensions are critical, so the materials box may be made to suit any particular spot you have to mount it, or any materials you may have on hand.

Birdseed Scoop

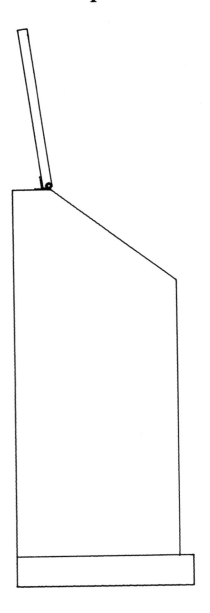

Illus. 113. Birdseed Scoop. This is readily made with tin snips, a used coffee can, a 6-inch piece of 1-inch diameter wood dowel, a #8 x 1¼-inch round-head wood screw, and about 10 or 15 minutes.

Cut the already open end of the coffee can as shown, drill a pilot hole in the end of the remaining can bottom, insert the wood screw—use a flat washer to aid durability—and screw the dowel on tight, for the handle.

If you wish, you can shape the dowel to fit your hand. For safety, you may wish to nip the sharp edge of the coffee can and use a ballpen hammer to bend that nipped edge back flat so the edge is safer. A strip of electrician's plastic tape also works.

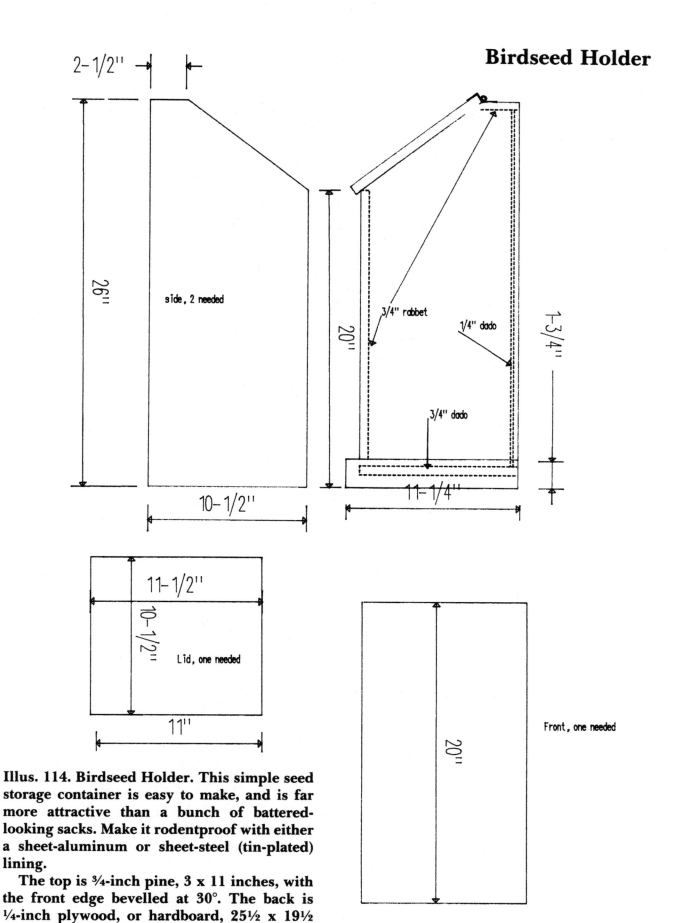

Illus. 114. Birdseed Holder. This simple seed storage container is easy to make, and is far more attractive than a bunch of battered-looking sacks. Make it rodentproof with either a sheet-aluminum or sheet-steel (tin-plated) lining.

The top is ¾-inch pine, 3 x 11 inches, with the front edge bevelled at 30°. The back is ¼-inch plywood, or hardboard, 25½ x 19½ inches.

Two-Bin Tilt-Out Seed Holder

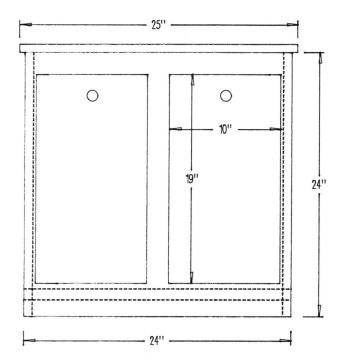

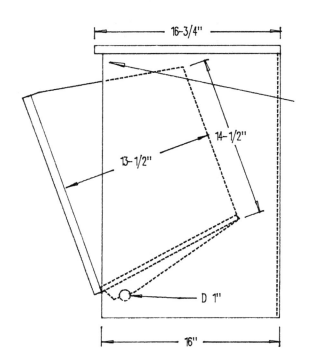

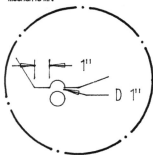

One inch dowel provides the tilt out mechanism.

Illus. 115. Two-Bin Tilt-Out Seed Holder. Sides, backs, and bottoms of bins must be made of ½-inch or thicker B-C plywood (face the B side into the bin to provide a smooth surface). Place a screwed-in wooden stop along the top of the sides of the bin frames to keep the bins from tilting too far out and depositing their contents on the floor. Make all grooves so that the direction of the load is against the wood, not against the glue or the nails alone. A 1-inch dowel provides the tilt-out mechanism.

The fronts of the bins must have at least ½-inch overhang on the frame. If a straight groove is used, a backboard the same thickness as the bin front is needed for good durability (¾ inch with the sides nailed or screwed into the backboard as well as glued into the groove). Alternatively, the groove may be a dovetail and simply glued.

Jointed Pole

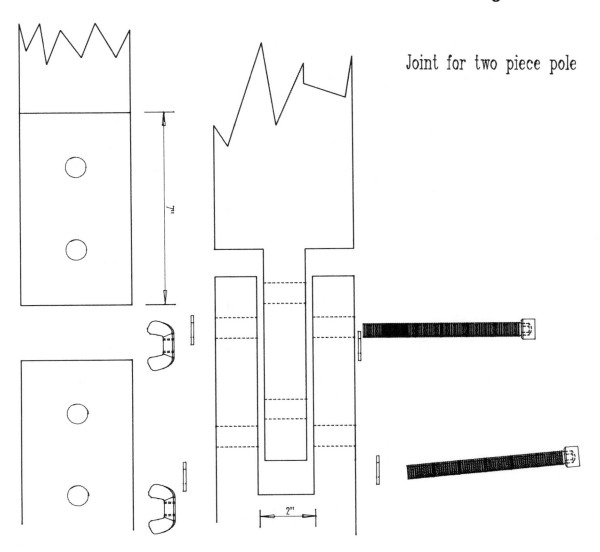

Joint for two piece pole

Illus. 116. Jointed Pole. In use, the pole, once erected, should not have both bolts totally removed at the same time.

If enough play has been left in the joint—¼ inch in each direction is maximum—removing only the bottom bolt will allow you to control the upper pole better. Using a long pole—a closet rod pole with a piece of 60-grit sandpaper glued to the top—makes erection simpler.

Do NOT stand directly under the upper part with a house or a feeder attached as the upper arm is lowered.

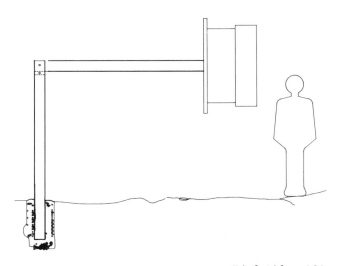

Pipe Flange

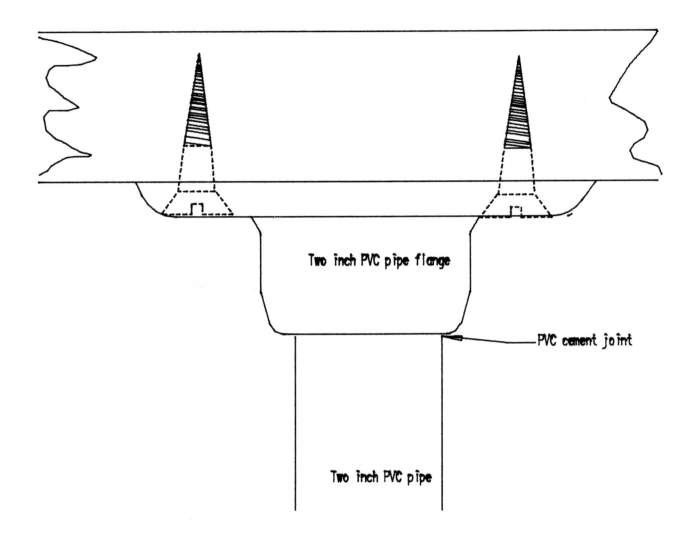

Two inch PVC pipe flange

PVC cement joint

Two inch PVC pipe

Illus. 117. Pipe Flange for Post Mount. Plastic pipe is recommended for two reasons: it is more readily available, generally; it is also much easier to work, with fewer tools and better results. Two-inch OD PVC pipe should be sufficient for all but the very largest and heaviest houses and feeders.

Eyebolt for Hanging Feeders

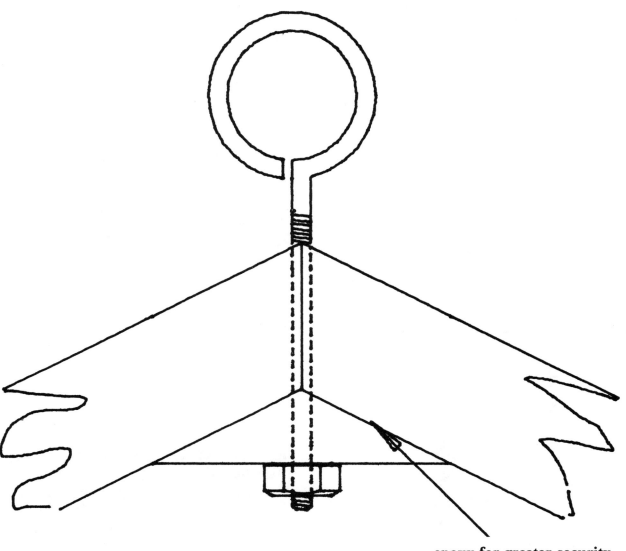

epoxy for greater security

Illus. 118. Eyebolt for Hanging Feeders and Houses. Note that the eyebolt runs through a brace-block cut to the inside roof angle. This brace need not be fastened in place with anything but the eyebolt nut and washer, and it will provide greater strength if a dab or two of epoxy is also used on each piece of the roof.

As scaled, this eyebolt starts with a ¼-inch screw shank, but scale upwards or downwards as any particular design requires. Eyebolt hangers work best in pairs, one near the front of the roof and one near the rear.

Birdbath

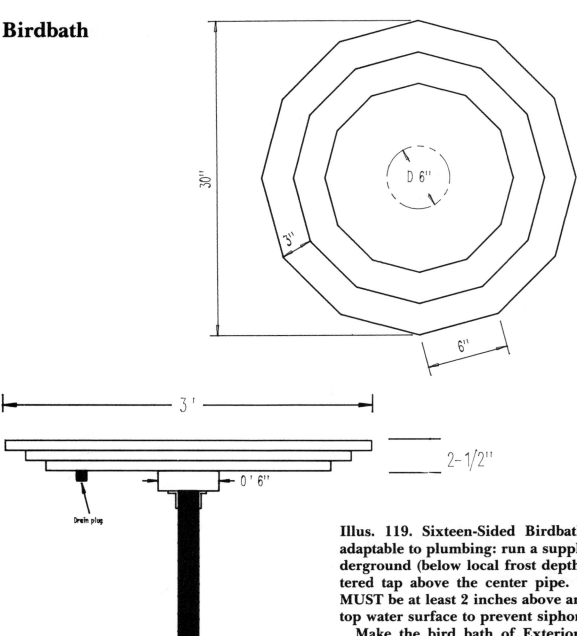

Illus. 119. Sixteen-Sided Birdbath. This is adaptable to plumbing: run a supply pipe underground (below local frost depth) to a centered tap above the center pipe. Tap outlet MUST be at least 2 inches above any possible top water surface to prevent siphoning.

Make the bird bath of Exterior plywood, using a 16-sided polygon pattern. Reduce size of piece #2 by 3 inches in diameter. Piece #3 is solid, except for the plug hole. The pipe and the pipe collar can be obtained in any building supply store from the DWV system supplies. Use 2-inch schedule 40.

The plug can be a push-in type, applied from above; in type of PVC or metal; or you may thread the wood.

The wood overlaps 1 inch. Overall depth of water will not exceed 1½ inches, allowing for some splashing. You can join pieces either of two ways: silicone seal or a top quality silicone-based house caulk and brass #6 x 1¼-inch (at longest) wood screws; or by using resorcinol wood glue.

Appendixes

Appendix A

The illustrations in this section are supplied by the Educational Division of Stanley Tools. It may be a bit strange to lift (with Stanley's permission) an entire subject, but the odds are good that any similar drawings and notes you may have seen were derived from these 1950 drawings for school use; and if they were not, they should have been. These cover the field as well as it can be covered in a short space, and redoing them would be nothing more than a form of mimicry. Thus, here they are.

COMMON WOOD JOINTS

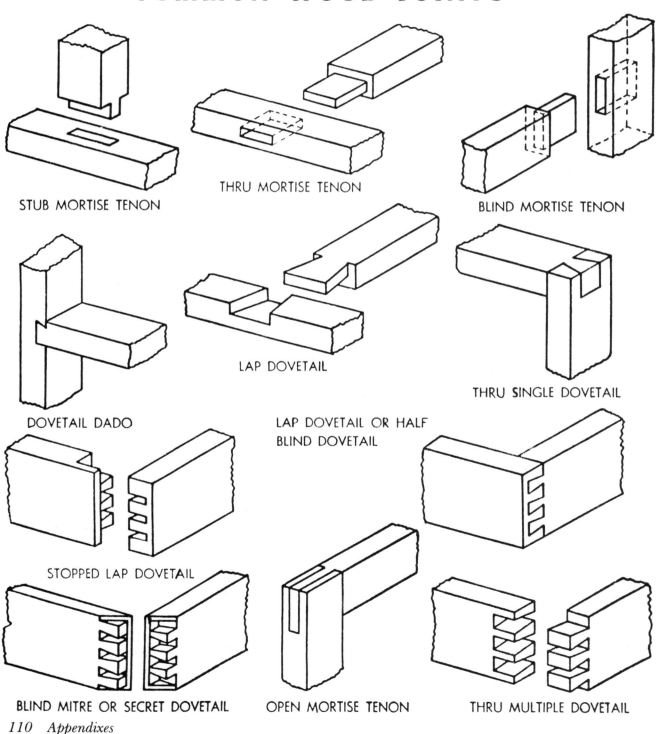

STUB MORTISE TENON

THRU MORTISE TENON

BLIND MORTISE TENON

DOVETAIL DADO

LAP DOVETAIL

THRU SINGLE DOVETAIL

STOPPED LAP DOVETAIL

LAP DOVETAIL OR HALF BLIND DOVETAIL

BLIND MITRE OR SECRET DOVETAIL

OPEN MORTISE TENON

THRU MULTIPLE DOVETAIL

HOW TO USE
THE STANLEY NAIL HAMMER

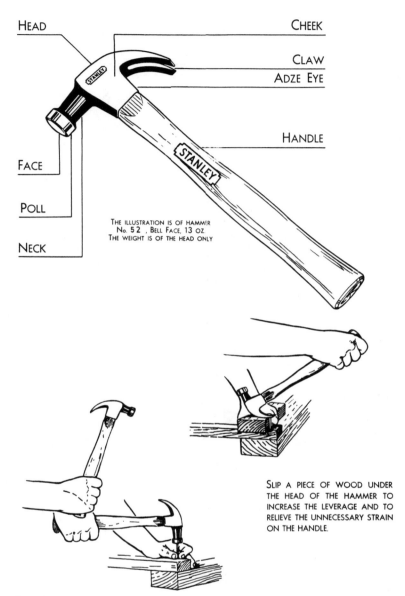

HEAD

CHEEK

CLAW

ADZE EYE

HANDLE

FACE

POLL

NECK

THE ILLUSTRATION IS OF HAMMER
No. 52, BELL FACE, 13 OZ.
THE WEIGHT IS OF THE HEAD ONLY

GRASP THE HAMMER FIRMLY NEAR THE END.

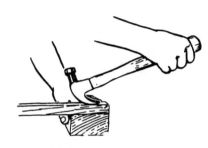

TO DRAW A NAIL: SLIP THE CLAW OF THE HAMMER UNDER THE NAIL HEAD; PULL UNTIL THE HANDLE IS NEARLY VERTICAL AND THE NAIL PARTLY DRAWN.

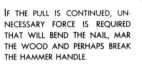

SLIP A PIECE OF WOOD UNDER THE HEAD OF THE HAMMER TO INCREASE THE LEVERAGE AND TO RELIEVE THE UNNECESSARY STRAIN ON THE HANDLE.

IF THE PULL IS CONTINUED, UN-NECESSARY FORCE IS REQUIRED THAT WILL BEND THE NAIL, MAR THE WOOD AND PERHAPS BREAK THE HAMMER HANDLE.

THE BLOW IS DELIVERED THROUGH THE WRIST, THE ELBOW AND THE SHOULDER, ONE OR ALL BEING BROUGHT INTO PLAY, ACCORDING TO THE STRENGTH OF THE BLOW TO BE STRUCK. REST THE FACE OF THE HAMMER ON THE NAIL, DRAW THE HAMMER BACK AND GIVE A LIGHT TAP TO START THE NAIL AND TO DETERMINE THE AIM.

STRIKE THE NAIL SQUARELY TO AVOID MARRING THE WOOD AND BENDING THE NAIL. KEEP THE FACE OF THE HAMMER CLEAN TO AVOID SLIPPING OFF THE NAIL. IF A NAIL BENDS DRAW IT AND START A NEW ONE IN A NEW PLACE.

ALWAYS STRIKE WITH THE FACE OF THE HAMMER IT IS HARDENED FOR THAT PURPOSE. DO NOT DAMAGE THE FACE BY STRIKING STEEL HARDER THAN ITSELF. DO NOT STRIKE WITH THE CHEEK AS IT IS THE WEAKEST PART.

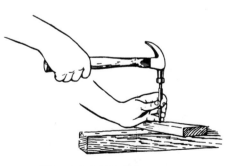

USE A NAIL SET TO DRIVE NAILS BELOW THE SURFACE OF ALL FINE WORK. TO PREVENT THE NAIL SET SLIPPING OFF THE HEAD OF THE NAIL, REST THE LITTLE FINGER ON THE WORK AND PRESS THE NAIL SET FIRMLY AGAINST IT. SET NAILS ABOUT 1/16" BELOW THE SURFACE OF THE WOOD.

HOW TO USE HAND SAWS

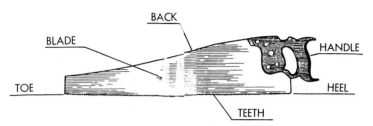

THE SIZE OF A SAW IS DETERMINED BY THE LENGTH OF THE BLADE IN INCHES. SOME POPULAR SIZES ARE 24" AND 26".

THE COARSENESS OR FINENESS OF A SAW IS DETERMINED BY THE NUMBER OF POINTS PER INCH.

A COARSE SAW IS BETTER FOR FAST WORK AND FOR GREEN WOOD.

A FINE SAW IS BETTER FOR SMOOTH ACCURATE CUTTING AND FOR DRY SEASONED WOOD.

5-1/2 AND 6 POINTS ARE IN COMMON USE FOR RIP SAWS.

7 AND 8 POINTS ARE IN COMMON USE FOR CROSS CUT SAWS.

SAW TEETH ARE SET; EVERY OTHER TOOTH IS BENT TO THE RIGHT AND THOSE BETWEEN TO THE LEFT, TO MAKE THE KERF WIDER THAN THE SAW.

THIS PREVENTS THE SAW FROM BINDING IN THE KERF OR SAW CUT.

QUALITY SAWS IN ADDITION ARE TAPER GROUND, BEING THINNER AT THE BACK THAN AT THE TOOTHED EDGE.

KEEP SAW TEETH SHARP AND PROPERLY SET.

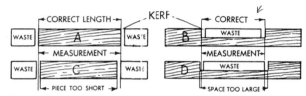

BE SURE TO SAW CAREFULLY ON THE WASTE SIDE OF THE LINE AS AT A AND B. SAWING ON THE LINE OR ON THE WRONG SIDE OF THE LINE MAKES THE STOCK TOO SHORT AS AT C OR THE OPENING TOO LARGE AS SHOWN AT D.

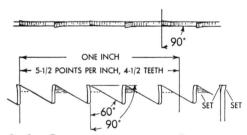

RIP SAW TEETH ARE SHAPED LIKE CHISELS. THEY CUT LIKE A GANG OF CHISELS IN A ROW.

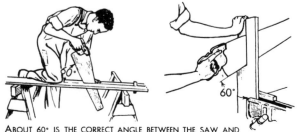

ABOUT 60° IS THE CORRECT ANGLE BETWEEN THE SAW AND THE WORK FOR RIP SAWING.

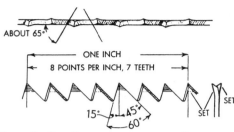

CROSS CUT SAW TEETH ARE LIKE KNIFE POINTS. THEY CUT LIKE TWO ROWS OF KNIFE POINTS AND CRUMBLE OUT THE WOOD BETWEEN THE CUTS.

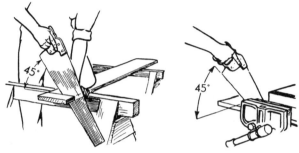

ABOUT 45° IS THE CORRECT ANGLE BETWEEN THE SAW AND THE WORK FOR CROSS CUT SAWING.

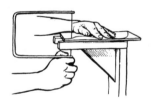 

THE COPING SAW IS USED TO CUT IRREGULAR SHAPES AND INTRICATELY CURVED PATTERNS IN THIN WOOD.

THE BACK SAW IS A THIN CROSS CUT SAW WITH FINE TEETH, STIFFENED BY A THICK BACK. A POPULAR SIZE IS 12" WITH 14 PTS PER INCH. IT IS USED FOR FINE ACCURATE WORK.

 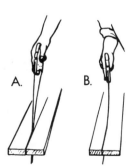

START THE SAW CUT BY DRAWING THE SAW BACKWARD. HOLD THE BLADE SQUARE TO THE STOCK. STEADY IT AT THE LINE WITH THE THUMB.

A. IF THE SAW LEAVES THE LINE TWIST THE HANDLE SLIGHTLY AND DRAW IT BACK TO THE LINE.
B. IF THE SAW IS NOT SQUARE TO THE STOCK, BEND IT A LITTLE AND GRADUALLY STRAIGHTEN IT. BE CAREFUL NOT TO PERMANENTLY BEND OR KINK THE BLADE.

HOW TO USE BORING TOOLS

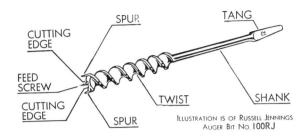

SPUR   TANG

CUTTING EDGE

FEED SCREW

CUTTING EDGE

SPUR   TWIST   SHANK

ILLUSTRATION IS OF RUSSELL JENNINGS AUGER BIT No. 100RJ

AUGER BITS ARE SIZED BY 16THS OF AN INCH, MEASURING THE DIAMETER. BITS VARY IN LENGTH FROM 7" TO 10". DOWEL BITS ARE SHORT AUGER BITS ABOUT 5" LONG.

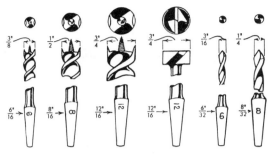

AUGER BITS, 16THS OF AN INCH   FORSTNER BITS 16THS.   TWIST BITS, 32NDS OF AN INCH.

BITS ARE MARKED FOR SIZE BY A SINGLE NUMBER. THE NUMERATOR OF THE FRACTION STANDS FOR THE DIAMETER OF THE BIT. AUGER AND FORSTNER BITS ARE MARKED BY 16THS OF AN INCH. No. 8 STANDS FOR 8/16" OR 1/2". TWIST BITS FOR WOOD ARE USUALLY MARKED IN THE SAME WAY, BY 32NDS OF AN INCH. No. 8 STANDS FOR 8/32" OR 1/4".

BRAD AWLS ARE USED TO MAKE HOLES FOR SMALL SCREWS AND NAILS. TO AVOID SPLITTING THE WOOD, START THE AWL WITH ITS EDGE ACROSS THE GRAIN, TURNING IT BACK AND FORTH SLIGHTLY AS YOU PRESS DOWN. DO NOT LET THE EDGE COME PARALLEL WITH THE GRAIN.

ILLUSTRATION IS OF STANLEY BIT GAUGE No. 47

AN ADJUSTABLE BIT GAUGE MAY BE USED TO REGULATE THE DEPTH OF HOLES.

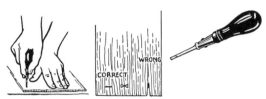

TWIST BITS FOR WOOD ARE USED TO MAKE HOLES FOR SCREWS, NAILS OR BOLTS. THEY ARE SIZED BY 32NDS OF AN INCH AND RANGE FROM No. 2=1/16" AND LARGER.

BIT STOCK DRILLS ARE DESIGNED AND TEMPERED TO MAKE HOLES IN METAL, BUT MAY ALSO BE USED IN WOOD, ESPECIALLY IN REPAIR WORK WHERE CONTACT WITH NAILS OR METAL IS POSSIBLE. THEY ARE SIZED BY 32NDS OF AN INCH AND RANGE FROM No. 2 = 1/16" AND LARGER.

ILLUSTRATION IS OF RUSSELL JENNINGS EXPANSIVE BIT No. 71

THE EXPANSIVE BIT TAKES THE PLACE OF MANY LARGE BITS. THE CUTTER MAY BE ADJUSTED FOR VARIOUS SIZED HOLES. MOVING THE CUTTER ADJUSTING SCREW ONE COMPLETE TURN ENLARGES OR REDUCES THE HOLE 1/8". ONE HALF TURN 1/16". TEST THE SIZE ON A PIECE OF WASTE WOOD. FOR BORING THROUGH, CLAMP A PIECE OF WASTE WOOD ON THE BACK OF THE WORK TO PREVENT SPLITTING.

ILLUSTRATION IS OF STANLEY COUNTERSINK No. 139 FOR BIT BRACES

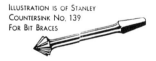

ILLUSTRATION IS OF STANLEY COUNTERSINK No. 137 FOR HAND DRILLS.

COUNTERSINK BITS ARE USED TO WIDEN SCREW HOLES SO THAT THE HEADS OF FLAT-HEAD SCREWS MAY BE FLUSH, OR SLIGHTLY BELOW, THE SURFACE OF THE WORK.

THE STANDARD DOUBLE THREAD FEED SCREW IS BEST FOR GENERAL WORK WITH SEASONED WOOD. IT IS PREFERRED FOR CABINET AND PATTERN MAKING.

THE SINGLE THREAD FEED SCREW IS BEST FOR FAST CUTTING IN GREEN OR GUMMY WOOD.

THE DIAMOND POINT IS USED FOR MACHINE BORING WITH POWER FEED.

FORSTNER BITS ARE USED TO BORE HOLES PARTWAY THROUGH WHERE THE AUGER BIT SCREW OR SPUR WOULD GO THROUGH THE WORK, ALSO ON END GRAIN, THIN WOOD, OR NEAR AN END WHERE AN AUGER BIT WOULD SPLIT THE WORK. TO CENTER OR START A FORSTNER BIT, SCRIBE A CIRCLE THE SIZE OF THE HOLE WITH DIVIDERS AND PRESS THE RIM OF THE FORSTNER BIT INTO IT. FORSTNER BITS ARE SIZED BY 16THS OF AN INCH FROM No. 4=1/4" AND LARGER.

SHARPEN AUGER BITS WITH A BIT FILE. FOR A KEEN EDGE, ALSO WHET WITH A SLIPSTONE. SHARPEN THE SPURS ON THE INSIDE TO PRESERVE THE DIAMETER.

SHARPEN THE CUTTING EDGES ON THE TOP TO MAINTAIN THE CLEARANCE ON THE UNDER SIDE. THE CUTTING EDGES MUST BE KEPT EVEN.

HOW TO USE
MEASURING AND MARKING TOOLS

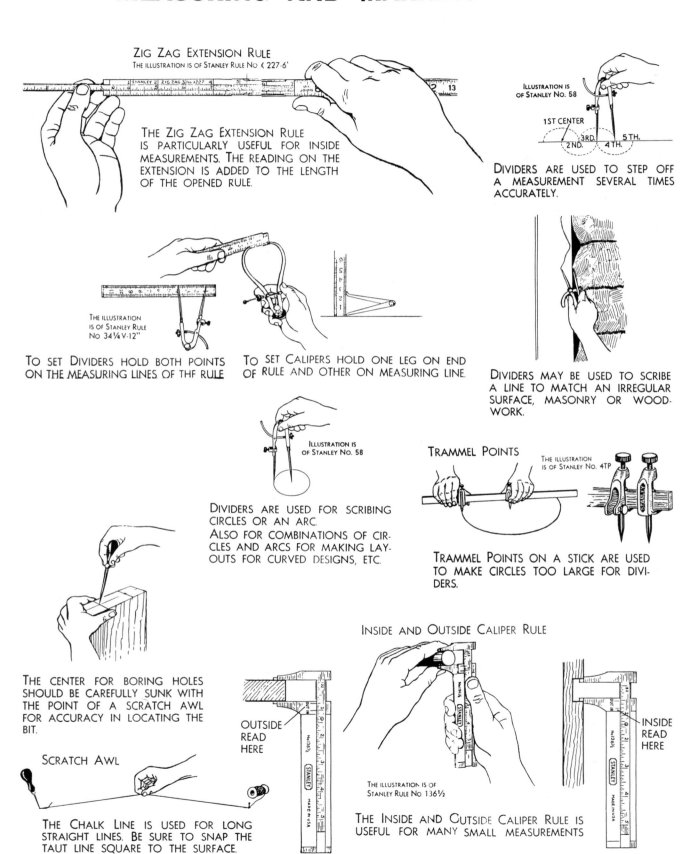

ZIG ZAG EXTENSION RULE
THE ILLUSTRATION IS OF STANLEY RULE NO ‹ 227-6'

THE ZIG ZAG EXTENSION RULE IS PARTICULARLY USEFUL FOR INSIDE MEASUREMENTS. THE READING ON THE EXTENSION IS ADDED TO THE LENGTH OF THE OPENED RULE.

ILLUSTRATION IS OF STANLEY NO. 58

1ST CENTER
2ND. 3RD. 4TH. 5TH.

DIVIDERS ARE USED TO STEP OFF A MEASUREMENT SEVERAL TIMES ACCURATELY.

THE ILLUSTRATION IS OF STANLEY RULE NO. 34 1/4 V-12"

TO SET DIVIDERS HOLD BOTH POINTS ON THE MEASURING LINES OF THE RULE

TO SET CALIPERS HOLD ONE LEG ON END OF RULE AND OTHER ON MEASURING LINE.

DIVIDERS MAY BE USED TO SCRIBE A LINE TO MATCH AN IRREGULAR SURFACE, MASONRY OR WOODWORK.

ILLUSTRATION IS OF STANLEY NO. 58

DIVIDERS ARE USED FOR SCRIBING CIRCLES OR AN ARC.
ALSO FOR COMBINATIONS OF CIRCLES AND ARCS FOR MAKING LAYOUTS FOR CURVED DESIGNS, ETC.

TRAMMEL POINTS

THE ILLUSTRATION IS OF STANLEY NO. 4TP

TRAMMEL POINTS ON A STICK ARE USED TO MAKE CIRCLES TOO LARGE FOR DIVIDERS.

THE CENTER FOR BORING HOLES SHOULD BE CAREFULLY SUNK WITH THE POINT OF A SCRATCH AWL FOR ACCURACY IN LOCATING THE BIT.

SCRATCH AWL

THE CHALK LINE IS USED FOR LONG STRAIGHT LINES. BE SURE TO SNAP THE TAUT LINE SQUARE TO THE SURFACE.

OUTSIDE READ HERE

INSIDE AND OUTSIDE CALIPER RULE

INSIDE READ HERE

THE ILLUSTRATION IS OF STANLEY RULE NO. 136 1/2

THE INSIDE AND OUTSIDE CALIPER RULE IS USEFUL FOR MANY SMALL MEASUREMENTS

COMMON CUTS IN WOOD

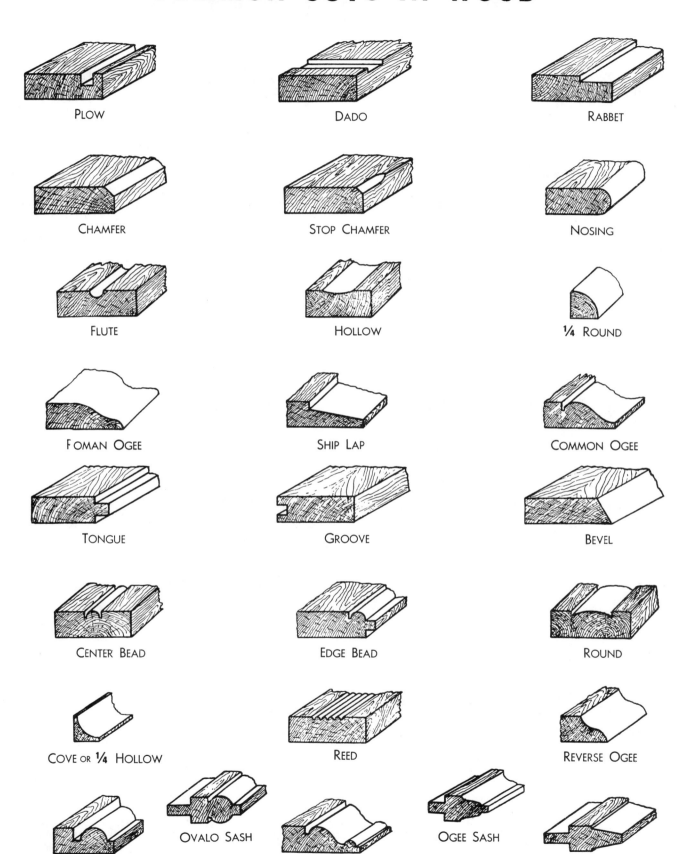

PLOW

DADO

RABBET

CHAMFER

STOP CHAMFER

NOSING

FLUTE

HOLLOW

¼ ROUND

FOMAN OGEE

SHIP LAP

COMMON OGEE

TONGUE

GROOVE

BEVEL

CENTER BEAD

EDGE BEAD

ROUND

COVE OR ¼ HOLLOW

REED

REVERSE OGEE

ASTRAGAL

OVALO SASH

GRECIAN OGEE WITH BEAD

OGEE SASH

BEVEL SASH

HOW TO USE
THE STANLEY BIT BRACE

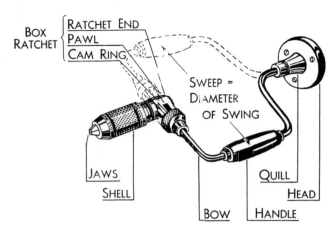

BOX RATCHET
RATCHET END
PAWL
CAM RING

SWEEP = DIAMETER OF SWING

JAWS
SHELL
BOW
HANDLE
QUILL
HEAD

THE ILLUSTRATION IS OF STANLEY RATCHET BIT BRACE NO. 923—10 IN. SWEEP

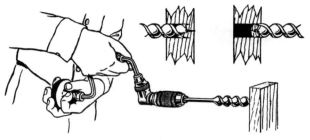

TO BORE A HORIZONTAL HOLE, HOLD THE HEAD OF THE BRACE CUPPED IN THE LEFT HAND AGAINST THE STOMACH AND WITH THE THUMB AND FOREFINGER AROUND THE QUILL. TO BORE THRU WITHOUT SPLINTERING THE SECOND FACE, STOP WHEN THE SCREW POINT IS THRU AND FINISH FROM THE SECOND FACE. WHEN BORING THRU WITH AN EXPANSIVE BIT IT IS BEST TO CLAMP A PIECE OF WOOD TO THE SECOND FACE AND BORE STRAIGHT THRU.

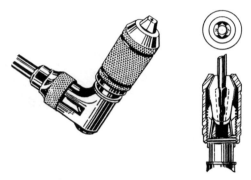

BIT BRACE CHUCKS OF THE ABOVE DESIGN, WITHOUT A SQUARE SOCKET ARE OPERATED IN LIKE MANNER. THE CORNERS OF THE TAPER SHANK OF THE BIT SHOULD BE CAREFULLY SEATED AND CENTERED IN THE V GROOVES OF THE JAWS.

TO OPERATE THE RATCHET TURN THE CAM RING. TURNING THE CAM RING TO THE RIGHT WILL ALLOW THE BIT TO TURN RIGHT AND GIVE RATCHET ACTION WHEN THE HANDLE IS TURNED LEFT. TURN THE CAM RING LEFT TO REVERSE THE ACTION.
THE RATCHET BRACE IS INDISPENSABLE WHEN BORING A HOLE IN A CORNER OR WHERE SOME OBJECT PREVENTS MAKING A FULL TURN WITH THE HANDLE.

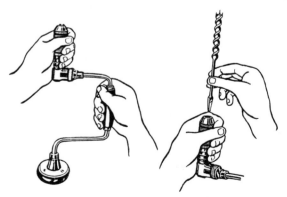

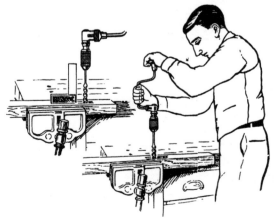

TO PLACE THE BIT IN THE CHUCK, GRASP THE CHUCK SHELL AND TURN THE HANDLE TO THE LEFT UNTIL THE JAWS ARE WIDE OPEN. INSERT THE BIT SHANK IN THE SQUARE SOCKET AT THE BOTTOM OF THE CHUCK AND TURN THE HANDLE TO THE RIGHT UNTIL THE BIT IS HELD FIRMLY IN THE JAWS.

TO BORE A VERTICLE HOLE, HOLD THE BRACE AND BIT PERPENDICULAR TO THE SURFACE OF THE WORK. TEST BY SIGHT. COMPARE THE DIRECTION OF THE BIT TO THE NEAREST STRAIGHT EDGE OR TO SIDES OF THE VISE. A TRY SQUARE MAY BE *HELD* NEAR THE BIT.

HOW TO USE
THE STANLEY HAND DRILL

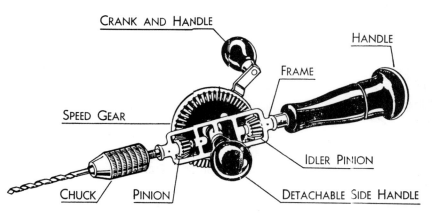

CRANK AND HANDLE

HANDLE

FRAME

SPEED GEAR

IDLER PINION

CHUCK   PINION

DETACHABLE SIDE HANDLE

THE ILLUSTRATION IS OF STANLEY HAND DRILL No. 624-⅜" CHUCK

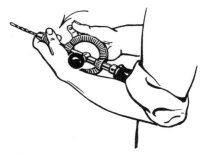

THE HAND DRILL IS USED FOR THE RAPID DRILLING OF SMALL HOLES, IN BOTH WOOD AND METAL. HOLES IN WOOD SHOULD BE STARTED WITH AN AWL TO HELP CENTER AND LOCATE THE DRILL. HOLES IN METAL SHOULD BE CENTER PUNCHED. WHEN DRILLING THROUGH METAL, RELIEVE THE PRESSURE SLIGHTLY BEFORE BREAKING THROUGH, TO AVOID BREAKING THE DRILL. TWIST DRILLS PRINCIPALLY FOR METAL ARE MADE IN A VAST RANGE OF SIZES.

TO PLACE THE DRILL IN THE CHUCK, OPEN IT ONLY SLIGHTLY MORE THAN THE DIAMETER OF THE DRILL. THIS HELPS TO CENTER IT. INSERT THE DRILL. TIGHTEN THE CHUCK BY PUSHING FORWARD ON THE CRANK WITH THE RIGHT HAND, WHILE HOLDING THE CHUCK SHELL TIGHT WITH THE LEFT THUMB AND FOREFINGER.

TO REMOVE THE DRILL, HOLD THE CHUCK SHELL TIGHT WITH THE LEFT THUMB AND FOREFINGER, AND TURN THE CRANK BACKWARD, WITH THE RIGHT HAND, AS SHOWN BY THE ARROW.

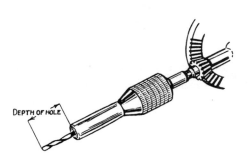

DEPTH OF HOLE

TO DRILL HOLES OF UNIFORM DEPTH, MAKE A DEPTH GAUGE. CUT A PIECE OF WOOD OR DOWEL THE RIGHT LENGTH, SO THE DRILL WILL PROJECT THE DESIRED DEPTH. WHEN THE PIECE OF WOOD IS DRILLED, SLIP IT OVER THE DRILL.

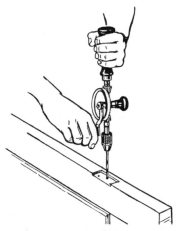

HOLD THE DRILL STEADY IN THE DIRECTION DESIRED AND EXERT AN EVEN PRESSURE. TURN THE CRANK AT A CONSTANT SPEED AND NOT TOO FAST.

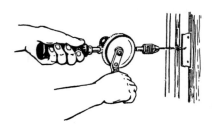

HOLD THE DRILL STRAIGHT. DO NOT WOBBLE WHILE TURNING, IT MAKES THE HOLE OVER-SIZE AND IS LIKELY TO BREAK THE DRILL.

IT IS SOME TIMES DESIRABLE TO HOLD THE DRILL BY THE SIDE HANDLE AND PRESS THE BODY AGAINST THE FRAME HANDLE LIKE A BREAST DRILL.

HOW TO USE
THE STANLEY TRY SQUARE
AND HOW TO SQUARE UP STOCK

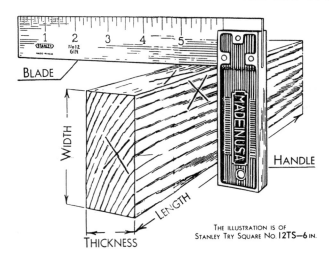

BLADE

WIDTH

LENGTH

THICKNESS

HANDLE

THE ILLUSTRATION IS OF
STANLEY TRY SQUARE No. 12TS—6 IN.

HOLD THE HANDLE OF THE TRY SQUARE TIGHT AGAINST THE STOCK WHEN TESTING ENDS, EDGES OR SCRIBING LINES. FOR THE USE OF THE MARKING GAUGE SEE STANLEY CHART NO. C8. FOR THE USE OF THE PLANE SEE STANLEY CHART NO. C14.

1. WORK FACE

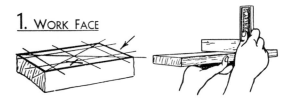

PLANE ONE BROAD SURFACE SMOOTH AND STRAIGHT. TEST IT CROSSWISE, LENGTHWISE, AND FROM CORNER TO CORNER. MARK THE WORK FACE X.

2. WORK EDGE

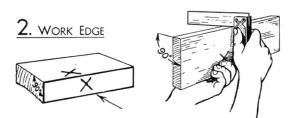

PLANE ONE EDGE SMOOTH, STRAIGHT AND SQUARE TO THE WORK FACE. TEST IT FROM THE WORK FACE. MARK THE WORK EDGE X.

3. WORK END

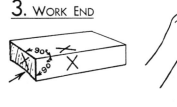

PLANE ONE END SMOOTH AND SQUARE. TEST IT FROM THE WORK FACE AND WORK EDGE. MARK THE WORK END X.

4. SECOND END

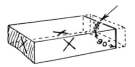

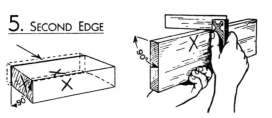

MEASURE LENGTH AND SCRIBE AROUND THE STOCK, A LINE SQUARE TO THE WORK EDGE AND WORK FACE. SAW OFF EXCESS STOCK NEAR THE LINE AND PLANE SMOOTH TO THE SCRIBED LINE. TEST THE SECOND END FROM BOTH THE WORK FACE AND THE WORK EDGE.

5. SECOND EDGE

FROM THE WORK EDGE GAUGE A LINE FOR WIDTH ON BOTH FACES. PLANE SMOOTH, STRAIGHT, SQUARE AND TO THE GAUGE LINE. TEST THE SECOND EDGE FROM THE WORK FACE.

6. SECOND FACE

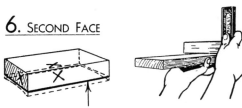

FROM THE WORK FACE GAUGE A LINE FOR THICKNESS AROUND THE STOCK. PLANE THE STOCK TO THE GAUGE LINE. TEST THE SECOND FACE AS THE WORK FACE IS TESTED.

118 Appendixes

HOW TO USE THE
STANLEY MARKING GAUGE

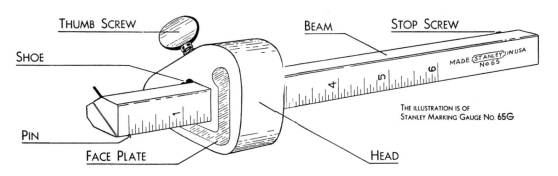

THUMB SCREW
SHOE
BEAM
STOP SCREW
PIN
FACE PLATE
HEAD

THE ILLUSTRATION IS OF
STANLEY MARKING GAUGE NO. 65G

MADE STANLEY IN USA No 65

HOLD THE GAUGE AS YOU WOULD A BALL.
ADVANCE THE THUMB TOWARD THE PIN SO AS TO DISTRIBUTE THE PRESSURE EVENLY BETWEEN THE PIN AND THE HEAD.

TO MAKE A GAUGE LINE PUSH THE GAUGE FORWARD WITH THE HEAD HELD TIGHT AGAINST THE WORK EDGE OF THE WOOD.
THE PRESSURE SHOULD BE APPLIED IN THE DIRECTION OF THE ARROWS.

THE PIN IS GROUND WITH A CONICAL POINT THEN ONE HALF IS GROUND FLAT. THIS GIVES A KNIFE TYPE LINE.

THE PIN SHOULD PROJECT ABOUT 1/16 IN. THE CURVED SIDE OF THE PIN HELPS TO KEEP IT FROM FOLLOWING THE GRAIN OF THE WOOD.

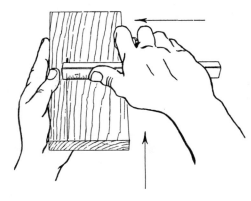

LAY THE BEAM FLAT ON THE WOOD SO THE PIN DRAGS NATURALLY AS THE MARKING GAUGE IS PUSHED AWAY. NO ROLL MOTION IS NECESSARY. THE PIN AND LINE ARE VISIBLE AT ALL TIMES.

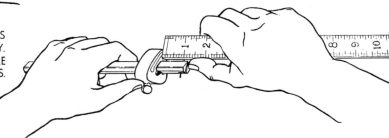

SET THE MARKING GAUGE BY MEASUREMENT FROM THE HEAD TO THE PIN. CHECK THE MEASUREMENT AFTER TIGHTENING THE THUMB SCREW.

Appendixes 119

Appendix B

Wood Suitability

Species	Locale	Characteristics & Uses
Ash	East of Rockies	Strong and heavy, with a tough, close, straight grain that takes a fine finish; ideal for making durable birdhouses.
Basswood	Eastern half of U.S., but not near coasts	Used mainly for low-grade furniture, basswood offers good workability but requires a durable finish.
Birch	East of Mississippi, southeastern Canada	Hard and durable, most birch is acceptable for making bird structures but does not withstand weathering well. Takes paint very well.
Butternut	Southern Canada, Minnesota, eastern U.S. to Alabama and Florida	A walnut-colored soft hardwood, though not as soft as basswood; easily worked, reasonably strong, with coarse grain; does not withstand weathering well.
Cypress	Maryland to Texas and along the Mississippi Valley to Indiana	Resembles white cedar, is water-resistant, very durable, usually expensive, and difficult to find.
Douglas fir	Pacific Coast and British Columbia	Strong, light, and clear-grained; tends to be brittle, but the heartwood is somewhat resistant to effects of weathering; readily available in most areas and moderately priced.
Hickory	Common from southern Virginia to New York, Ohio, Tennessee, and Kentucky	A very heavy, hard, and tough wood; tends to check and shrink; is hard to work and doesn't resist insects or decay well; easy to locate in much of the East, but nearly impossible to find in the West; expensive and difficult to use for making bird structures; use only if you have it on hand.
Live oak	Common along the coasts of Oregon, California, and the southern Atlantic and Gulf states	Heavy, hard, tough, strong, and durable; hard to work, but otherwise nearly perfect for most bird structures.
Maple	All states east of Colorado; southern Canada	Heavy, tough, strong, fairly easy to work but not durable, although a fine wood for birdhouses; may be expensive because it's hard to find in certain areas; different varieties offer different properties; rock, or sugar, maple is the hardest and most popular.
Norway pine	States bordering the Great Lakes	Light-colored, moderately hard softwood; not durable; fairly easy to work.
Poplar	Virginia, West Virginia, Tennessee, Kentucky, and along the Mississippi Valley	Soft, cheap hardwood; easily obtainable in wide boards because of rapid, straight tree growth; rots quickly if not protected but works easily and is finely textured.

Species	Locale	Characteristics & Uses
Red cedar	East of Colorado and north of Florida	Very, very light, soft, weak, and brittle wood with great durability, works easily; is hard to find and costly in wide-board form; excellent for birdhouses.
Red oak	Virginia, West Virginia, Tennessee, Arkansas, Kentucky, Ohio, Missouri, Maryland, and parts of New York	A coarse-grained, easily warped wood that doesn't last long; avoid outdoor uses.
Redwood	California	Ideal for birdhouses but expensive; not as strong as yellow pine; shrinks and splits only a little; is straight-grained and exceptionally durable without any finish; many inexpensive grades are available.
Spruce	New York, New England, West Virginia, the Great Lakes states, Idaho, Washington, Oregon, and through much of central Canada	A light, soft, fairly durable wood with close grain; makes good bird structures.
White cedar	Eastern coast of the United States and around the Great Lakes	A soft, light, close-grained wood, exceedingly durable and nearly ideal for birdhouses.
White oak	Virginia, West Virginia, Tennessee, Arkansas, Kentucky, Ohio, Missouri, Maryland, and Indiana	Heavy, hard, strong, with a moderately coarse-grain pattern; tough and dense; the most durable of all North American native hardwoods, fairly easy to work except for a tendency to check and shrink; may be expensive in some areas.
White pine	Minnesota, Wisconsin, Maine, Michigan, Idaho, Montana, Washington, Oregon, California, and in stands in some eastern states other than Maine	A fine-grained, easily worked wood that can sometimes be found with few knots; durable, soft, but not very strong, more than suitable for birdhouses; economical in most communities.
Yellow pine	Virginia to Texas; several species are classified as southern pine, which are somewhat knottier and harder to work than white pine	Hard, tough softwood; heartwood is durable with the grain; hard to nail; saws easily; an inexpensive and excellent wood for bird structures.

Appendix C

Approximate Number of Wire Nails per Pound (Theoretical Average)

Steel Wire Gauge	LENGTH — INCHES																					
	3/16	1/4	3/8	1/2	5/8	3/4	7/8	1	1⅛	1¼	1½	1¾	2	2¼	2½	2¾	3	3½	4	4½	5	6
2								60	54	48	41	35	31	28	25	23	21	18	16	14	13	11
3								67	60	55	47	41	36	32	29	27	25	21	18	16	15	12
4								81	74	66	55	48	41	37	34	31	29		24		18	15
5								90	81	74	61	52	45	41	38	35	32	28	24	22	21	18
6				213	174	149	128	113	101	91	76	65	58	52	47	43	39	34	29	26	24	20
7				250	205	174	148	132	120	110	92	78	70	61	55	53	51	40	35	31	28	24
8				272	238	198	174	153	139	126	106	93	82	74	66	61	56	48	42	38	34	28
9				348	286	238	213	185	170	152	128	112	99	87	79	71	67	58	50	45	44	34
10				469	373	320	277	242	216	196	165	142	124	111	100	91	84	71	62	55	49	42
11				510	417	366	323	285	254	233	200	171	149	136	122	111	103	87	77	69	61	52
12				740	603	511	442	405	351	327	268	229	204	182	161	149	137	118	103	95	87	71
13			1356	1017	802	688	590	508	458	412	348	294	260	232	209	190	175	153	138	123	110	93
14		2293	1664	1290	1037	863	806	667	610	536	459	406	350	312	278	256	233	201	176	157	140	117
15		2890	2213	1619	1316	1132	971	869	787	694	578	501	437	390	351	317	290	246	220	196	177	145
16		3932	2720	2142	1708	1414	1229	1090	973	872	739	635	553	496	452	410	370	318	277	248	226	
17		5316	3890	2700	2303	1904	1581	1409	1253	1139	956	831	746	666	590	532	486	418	360	322	295	
18		7520	5072	3824	3130	2608	2248	1976	1760	1590	1338	1150	996	890	820	740	680	585	507	448	412	
19		9920	6860	5075	4132	3508	2816	2556	2284	2096	1772	1590	1390	1205	1060	970	895	800				
20	18620	14050	9432	7164	5686	4795	4230	3596	3225	2893	2412	2070	1810	1620	1450	1315	1215	1435				

Penny Size Conversion Chart

Nail length is often designated by penny (d) size. The letter "d" is the English symbol for pound. It also means penny in the English monetary system. The theory is that penny size represented the number of pounds a thousand nails weighed. Today this antiquated system represents only the length of nails. It does **NOT** indicate count per pound, diameter, style and size head, or other characteristics.

PENNY SIZE	2d	3d	4d	5d	6d	7d	8d	9d	10d	12d
LENGTH — INCHES	1"	1¼"	1½"	1¾"	2"	2¼"	2½"	2¾"	3"	3¼"

PENNY SIZE	16d	20d	30d	40d	50d	60d	70d	80d	90d	100d
LENGTH — INCHES	3½"	4"	4½"	5"	5½"	6"	7"	8"	9"	10"

Color-Coded Blister Pak Nails

STOCK NUMBER	PIECES	COLOR CODE	DESCRIPTION
HMC-000	30	Yellow	★ ¾" Concrete Screw Nails - Helyx™
HMC-010	24	Yellow	★ 1" Concrete Screw Nails - Helyx™
HMC-020	18	Yellow	★ 1½" Concrete Screw Nails - Helyx™
HMC-030	14	Yellow	★ 2" Concrete Screw Nails - Helyx™
HMC-040	12	Yellow	★ 2½" Concrete Screw Nails - Helyx™
HMC-050	10	Yellow	★ 3" Concrete Screw Nails - Helyx™
HMC-100	30	Blue	★ ¾" Masonry Nails
HMC-110	24	Blue	★ 1" Masonry Nails
HMC-120	16	Blue	★ 1½" Masonry Nails
HMC-130	14	Blue	★ 2" Masonry Nails
HMC-140	12	Blue	★ 2½" Masonry Nails
HMC-150	10	Blue	★ 3" Masonry Nails
HMC-200	12	Pink	★ 8D (2½") Furring Nails - Hard Cut
HMC-300	44	Purple	1¾" x .083 Wood Siding Nails - Ring-Barb™, Electro-Galvanized
HMC-400	40	Orange	1¼" x .083 Underlay Nails - Ring-Barb™
HMC-500	20	Red	2" x No. 5 Underlay Screw Nails - Helyx™
HMC-600	16	Aqua	2½" x No. 6 Drive Screw Nails - Helyx™
HMC-700	26	Olive Green	1⅜" x .105 Drywall Nails - Ring-Barb™
HMC-800	20	Green	2½" x No. 5 Flooring Screw Nails - Helyx™
HMC-900	20	Tan	2½" x .115 Flooring Nails - Rol-Thread™, Hard

Made by Hillwood Manufacturing Co. and available from local hardware dealers.

Appendix D

Birdhouse Size Requirements

Types	Floor Size in Inches	Entry-Hole Size in Inches	Hole above Floor in Inches	Interior Depth in Inches	Nest above Ground in Feet
Bluebirds Eastern and Western	5 × 5	1½	6	8	5–10
Chickadees black-capped, Carolina, gray-headed Boreal & chestnut-backed	4 × 4	1⅛	6–8	8–10	6–15
Finch house	6 × 6	2	4	6	8–12
Flycatchers great-crested, olivaceous, Western	6 × 6	2	6–8	8–10	8–20
Nuthatches white-breasted, red-breasted	4 × 4	1¼	6–8	8–10	5–20
brown-headed	2 × 3	1	6–8	8–10	5–20
Owls barn	10 × 18	6	4	15–18	12–18
screech	8 × 8	3	9–12	12–15	10–30
barred	13 × 15	8	—	16	10–30
Phoebes Eastern and black	6 × 6	open, one side	—	6	8–12
Sparrows song	6 × 6	open, all sides	—	6	1–3
house	4 × 4	1½	6–8	8–10	4–12
Swallows barn		open, one side	—	6	8–12
purple martin	6 × 6	2½	1	6	15–20
tree	5 × 5	1½	1–5	6	10–15
Thrushes (American robin)	6 × 8	open, one side	—	8	6–15
Titmice plain, tufted, and bridled	4 × 4	1¼	6–8	8–10	6–15
Warbler prothonary	4 × 4	1½	5	8	4–7

Types	Floor Size in Inches	Entry-Hole Size in Inches	Hole above Floor in Inches	Interior Depth in Inches	Nest above Ground in Feet
Woodpeckers					
downy	4 × 4	1¼	6–8	8–10	6–20
flicker	7 × 7	2½	14–16	16–18	6–20
hairy	6 × 6	1½	9–12	12–15	12–20
redheaded	6 × 6	2	9–12	12–15	12–20
pileated	8 × 8	3–4	10–12	12–30	12–60
red-bellied	6 × 6	2½	10–12	12–14	12–20
Wrens					
brown-throated	4 × 4	1	1–6	6–8	6–10
Carolina	4 × 4	1⅛	1–6	6–8	6–10
house	4 × 4	1	1–6	6–8	6–10
winter	4 × 4	1 × 2½	4–6	6–8	5–10

As you can see, not a great deal of wood is required for any birdhouse. The exceptions are houses for woodpeckers and owls. Even birdhouses that are larger than usual require a small amount of wood.

Note, too, that as little as one foot in hanging height can make a big difference in the birds you attract. If you desire winter wrens, for instance, one less foot in height will help keep out other wrens.

Make certain that all entry holes 1½ inches and smaller in diameter are sized exactly in order to keep starlings out.

Appendix E

Metric Conversion Chart

UNIT	ABBREVIATION		APPROXIMATE U.S. EQUIVALENT		
Length					
		Number of Metres			
myriametre	mym	10,000	6.2 miles		
kilometre	km	1000	0.62 mile		
hectometre	hm	100	109.36 yards		
dekametre	dam	10	32.81 feet		
metre	m	1	39.37 inches		
decimetre	dm	0.1	3.94 inches		
centimetre	cm	0.01	0.39 inch		
millimetre	mm	0.001	0.04 inch		
Area					
		Number of Square Metres			
square kilometre	sq km *or* km²	1,000,000	0.3861 square miles		
hectare	ha	10,000	2.47 acres		
are	a	100	119.60 square yards		
centare	ca	1	10.76 square feet		
square centimetre	sq cm *or* cm²	0.0001	0.155 square inch		
Volume					
		Number of Cubic Metres			
dekastere	das	10	13.10 cubic yards		
stere	s	1	1.31 cubic yards		
decistere	ds	0.10	3.53 cubic feet		
cubic centimetre	cu cm *or* cm³ *also* cc	0.000001	0.061 cubic inch		
Capacity					
		Number of Litres	*Cubic*	*Dry*	*Liquid*
kilolitre	kl	1000	1.31 cubic yards		
hectolitre	hl	100	3.53 cubic feet	2.84 bushels	
dekalitre	dal	10	0.35 cubic foot	1.14 pecks	2.64 gallons
litre	l	1	61.02 cubic inches	0.908 quart	1.057 quarts
decilitre	dl	0.10	6.1 cubic inches	0.18 pint	0.21 pint
centilitre	cl	0.01	0.6 cubic inch		0.338 fluidounce
millilitre	ml	0.001	0.06 cubic inch		0.27 fluidram
Mass and Weight					
		Number of Grams			
metric ton	MT *or* t	1,000,000	1.1 tons		
quintal	q	100,000	220.46 pounds		
kilogram	kg	1,000	2.2046 pounds		
hectogram	hg	100	3.527 ounces		
dekagram	dag	10	0.353 ounce		
gram	g *or* gm	1	0.035 ounce		
decigram	dg	0.10	1.543 grains		
centigram	cg	0.01	0.154 grain		
milligram	mg	0.001	0.015 grain		

American Term	British Term
rabbet	rebate
finishing nail	lost head nail
flathead screw	countersink screw
screw eye	wood screw with ringed shank

Index

Numerals in italic refer to illustrations.

A-frame, *49*
AccuJoint, 36, 37
Adhesives, 9
American terms vs. British terms, 126
Ash, 120
Auxiliary fence, 38–39

Band saws, *17–19*
Barn swallow, 42
Basswood, 120
Bayonet saws, *23–24*
Birch, 120
Bird aid
   birdseed holders, *103–104*
   birdseed scoop, *102*
   eyebolt for hanging feeders and houses, *107*
   jointed pole, *105*
   nesting materials box, *101*
   pipe flange for post mount, *106*
   sixteen-sided birdbath, *108*
   squirrel and predator guard, *100*
Bird feeder designs
   finger-jointed, *85*
   flying wing ground, *82–83*
   four-way, *94*
   hanging, *95*
   hexagon-based, *86*
   hopper, *87*
   large hopper, *87*
   pagoda-style, *98*
   pentagon, *90*
   quick covered, *83*
   shed, *96–97*
   simple ground, *82*
   simple wind vane, *91*
   suet, *84*
   thistle, *88*
   wind vane, *92–93*
   windowsill, *89*
Bird feeds, 43–46
Birdseed holder, *103*
   two bin tilt-out, *104*
Birdseed scoop, *102*
Birdbath, sixteen-sided, *108*
Birdhouse designs
   chickadee house, *56–57*
   columned martin house, *62–63*
   crazy roof, *58*
   cupola, *61*
   flicker house, *59*
   flycatcher house, *52*
   A-frame, *49*
   gambrel roof nuthatch house, *70–71*
   gingerbread Victorian, *68–69*
   log cabin, *72*
   martin castle, *73*
   martin house, *54–55*
   nesting box, *50*
   New England salt box, *77–79*
   octagonal, *53*
   Old West saloon, *74–76*
   one-storey chalet, *66*
   shingled, *64–65*
   simple A-frame, *48*
   swing front flicker house, *60*

   titmouse house, *51*
   two-storey chalet, *67*
Birdhouse size requirements, 124–125
Bit brace, *30, 116*
Blue jay, 41
Bluebirds, 41
   birdhouse size requirements, 124
Boring tools, how to use, *113*
Brass screws, 10
British terms vs. American terms, 126
Bushtit, 41–42
Butternut, 120

Cardinals, 41
Cedar, 6, 121
Chalet
   one-storey, *66*
   two-storey, *67*
Chickadee, 42
   birdhouse size requirements, 124
   house, *56–57*
Chisels, *34*
Circular saw, *24*
Claw hammers, 28–29
Columned martin house, *62–63*
Coping saw, 28
Corn, 45
Crazy roof birdhouse, *58*
Cupola, *61*
Cut-off jig, 38, *40*
Cuts in wood, common, *115*
Cypress, 120

Douglas fir, 120
Dowels, 10
Drill press, *21*
Drills, 24–25, 29–30

Eyebolt for hanging feeders and houses, *107*

Finch, 42
   birdhouse size requirements, 124
Finger-Jointed Feeder, *85*
Finishes, 10–12
Flicker, 42
   house, *59*
Flycatcher
   birdhouse size requirements, 124
   house, *52*
Flying wing ground feeder, *82–83*
Folding rules, *31*
Four-way feeder, *94*

Gambrel roof nuthatch house, *70–71*
Gingerbread Victorian, *68–69*
Glue, 9
Goldfinch, 41
Grit, 46
Grosbeak, 41

Hacksaw, *28*
Hammers, 28–29, *111*
Hand drills, *117*
Handsaws, *28*, 112
Hand tools, 27–34. *See also specific tools*

Hanging birdhouses, eyebolt for, *107*
Hanging feeder, *95*
  eyebolt for, *107*
Hexagon-base covered feeder, *86*
Hickory, 6, 120
Hinges, 10
Hopper feeder, *87*

Jigs and aids, *35–40*
Jointed pole, *105*
Jointers, 22
Joints, common, *110*
Junco, 41

Large hopper feeder, *87*
Levels, *32–33*
Log cabin, *72*

Maple, 120
Marking gauge, *119*
Martin, 42
  castle, *73*
  columned house, *62–63*
  house, *54–55*
Materials, *5–112*
Measuring and marking tools, *31–33, 114*
Metric conversion chart, 126
Millet, 45
Milo, 45
Mitre boxes, *33*
Mitre gauge board clamp, *40*

Nails, 9
  color-coded blister pak, 123
  length, 122
  per pound, 122
Natural woods, 6–7
Nesting box, *50*
Nesting materials box, *101*
New England salt box, *77–79*
Nuthatch, 42
  birdhouse size requirements, 124
  house, gambrel roof, *70–71*

Oak, 120, 121
Octagonal birdhouse, *53*
Old West saloon, *10, 74–76*
One-story chalet, *66*
Oriole, 42
Owls, birdhouse size requirements, 124

Pagoda-Style Feeder, *98*
Palm sander, *11*
Panel saws, 28
Penny size conversion chart, 122
Pentagon feeder, *90*
Phillips screwhead, 10
Phoebes, birdhouse size requirements, 124
Pine, 6–7, 120, 121
Pipe flange for post mount, *106*
Planer, *26*
Planes, *33–34*
Plastic, 10
Poplar, 120
Post mount, pipe flange for, *106*
Power mitre saws, *26*
Power tools, *13–26*
  portable, *22–26*
  stationary, *13–22*
Predator guard, *100*
Pressure-treated wood, 5–6
Push stick, *40*

Quick covered feeder, *83*

Reciprocating saw, *25*
Redwood, *5*, 6, 121
Resorcinol adhesive, 9
Rip fence, 38
Robertson screwhead, 10
Robin, 42
  birdhouse size requirements, 124
Router jigs, 37
Routers, *8, 22–23*

Saw blades, 39
Saws, hand, *28*
Scratch feed, 46
Screwdrivers, 29
Screws, 10
Scroll saws, *20*
Self-tapping screws, 10
Shed feeder, *96–97*
Shingled birdhouse, *64–65*
Shop helper, *36–37*
Simple A-frame, *48*
Simple ground feeder, *82*
Simple wind vane feeder, *91*
Sixteen-sided birdbath, *108*
Size requirements, for birdhouse, 124–125
Soft hammers, 29
Sorghum, 45
Southern pine, 6–7
Sparrows, birdhouse size requirements, 124
Spruce, 121
Squares, *32*
Squaring up stock, *118*
Squirrel and predator guard, *100*
Stainless steel screws, 10
Suet, 46
Suet feeder, *84*
Sunflower seed, 44
Swallows, birdhouse size requirements, 124
Swing front flicker house, *60*

Table saw jigs, *37–39*
Table saws, *13–17*, 39
Taper jig, 38
Tenoning jig, *39*
Thistle, 45
Thistle feeder, *44*, 88
Thrushes, birdhouse size requirements, 124
Titmouse
  birdhouse size requirements, 124
  house, *51*
Towhee, 43
Try square, *118*
Tufted titmouse, 42–43
Two bin tilt-out seed holder, *104*
Two story chalet, *67*

Utility knife, *32*

Waferboard, 8
Waferwood, 8
Warbler, birdhouse size requirements, 124
Wheat, 45
White pine, 6, 7
Wind vane feeder, *92–93*
  simple, *91*
Windowsill feeder, *89*
Wood
  manufactured, 7–8
  natural, 6–7
  pressure-treated, 5–6
  suitability of, 120–121
Woodpecker, 43
  birdhouse size requirements, 125
Wren, 43
  birdhouse size requirements, 125